The Best Book
on the Market

The Best Book on the Market

How to stop worrying and love the free economy

Eamonn Butler
Director, Adam Smith Institute

CAPSTONE
be inspired!
™

Other Wiley Editorial Offices

John Wiley & Sons Inc., 111 River Street, Hoboken, NJ 07030, USA
Jossey-Bass, 989 Market Street, San Francisco, CA 94103-1741, USA
Wiley-VCH Verlag GmbH, Boschstr. 12, D-69469 Weinheim, Germany
John Wiley & Sons Australia Ltd, 42 McDougall Street, Milton, Queensland 4064, Australia
John Wiley & Sons (Asia) Pte Ltd, 2 Clementi Loop #02-01, Jin Xing Distripark,
Singapore 129809
John Wiley & Sons Canada Ltd, 22 Worcester Road, Etobicoke, Ontario, Canada M9W 1L1

Wiley also publishes its books in a variety of electronic formats. Some content that appears in print may
not be available in electronic books.

Library of Congress Cataloging-in-Publication Data

Butler, Eamonn.
    The best little book on the market : how to stop worrying and love the free economy / Eamonn Butler.
    p. cm.
    Includes index.
    ISBN 978-1-906465-05-6 (pbk.)
1. Free enterprise.   2. Entrepreneurship.   3. Competition.   I. Title.
    HB95.B88 2008
    330.12'2 – dc22

                                                                                            2008007650

A catalogue record for this book is available from the British Library.

ISBN 13: 978-1-90646-505-6

Typeset by SNP Best-set Typesetter Ltd., Hong Kong
Printed and bound in TJ International, Padstow, Cornwall

Substantial discounts on bulk quantities of Capstone Books are available to corporations, professional
associations and other organizations. For details telephone John Wiley & Sons on (+44) 1243 770441, fax
(+44) 1243 770571 or email corporatedevelopment@wiley.co.uk

Contents

Acknowledgements

My thanks go to Anthony Haynes, for suggesting this project; to Christine Butler for her patience during its execution; and to Madsen Pirie and Cosmo Butler for their helpful suggestions on the text.

'Market' is one of the first six words that every English-speaking child learns: as in 'This – little – piggy – went – to – market.'

– Former UK Chancellor of the Exchequer
Lord (Geoffrey) Howe

CHAPTER ONE

The Amazing World of Markets

A TRIP TO THE MARKET

Few Westerners visit the dusty industrial city of Lanzhou, on China's Yellow River. Even fewer venture up the narrow dirt road that I am on today – which is home to one of the city's street markets. It is lined with stalls, their thin wooden poles supporting roofs and walls of dingy fabric. From beside one of them, a small boy stares at me in amazement, then runs in excitedly to report this strange sight to his mother.

She sits, by a spring balance twice her age, in the cramped space that remains behind all her stock: sacks of rice, grain, sunflower seeds and nuts, and above them a rickety shelf crowded with bags full of brightly-coloured spices – which prospective customers are sniffing and tasting, before checking out the next dry-goods stall.

Plastic baths of water, full of live fish,
jut into my path.

The boy still stares, still goggle-eyed. But I press on purposefully. The next stall is piled high with melons, bananas, pomegranates, limes, ginger, leeks, potatoes, beans, maize, cauliflowers and strange vegetables. The stallholder, a young woman with long black hair, is scrubbing one such vegetable over an enamel bowl full of water.

A bell rings behind me. I move smartly out of the way of a bicycle pulling a steaming brazier, the size of an oil drum, from which its owner sells hot soup.

I walk on. Plastic baths of water, full of live fish, jut into my path. Next, there's a stall with wooden cages full of live chickens, ducks and pigeons. Then more fish, this time in steel pans. Then someone selling underwear. Next, a hardware stall with countless woks, earthenware jars, glasses, rice-bowls in tottering stacks, brushes of all shapes and colours, dustpans, buckets and more. A second bell heralds another bicycle, this one carrying a precarious pile of squashed-up cardboard boxes that someone is taking for recycling, all bearing Chinese lettering in garish colours. Meanwhile, smoke drifts across from a stall with hot food (it's best not to ask what) sizzling on a gas stove that is well past pension age. Another stall offers cakes of various sizes and colours, nestling incongruously alongside sausages, hens' feet, rolled meat, fishcakes and balls of – well, again, I am not really sure that I want to know.

NO WORDS, BUT MUTUAL BENEFIT

I have reached my goal: a tiny wooden kiosk with no door and a large unglazed window. Inside sits a young, attractive girl in a red shirt, the street market's only seamstress. She has no sewing machine – though one day, perhaps, she will have saved enough to buy one – but she stitches by hand with great precision.

We cannot speak each other's language, but I hand her the slacks that I am holding, and show her how the hems have come adrift. She grasps my meaning immediately, and nods exaggeratedly – as if to make plain, even to someone unlucky enough not to be born Chinese, that she understands. I want to know the price: so I point to my palm with a puzzled expression on my face. She holds up five fingers, which I guess means five Yuan. That's probably way over the going rate, but to me it's a tiny sum and I would much rather pay it than waste time looking for another seamstress.

> **Barefoot children gather to stare**
> **at this strange creature.**

I nod. The slacks are plucked from my hand, out comes the needle and – worryingly – some rather garish pink thread. I stand outside – there is no room for two in her small workspace – and look around as I wait. Further from the main thoroughfare, the stalls give way to people selling fruit, vegetables, oil, rice – even underwear – from carts. Further still, vendors sit on the ground, their goods spread out on a simple sheet.

Barefoot children gather to stare at this strange creature that has landed among them. But within minutes, my hems are neatly stitched, without a speck of pink thread to be seen. I gladly pay the agreed fee, and leave with much mutual smiling and nodding. I seem to have made her day – though I hope it's because I'm exotic, not because I have overpaid. And she has made mine: I can now attend my evening banquet without safety pins in my hems.

I have learned a lot, too.

MARKETS ARE EVERYWHERE

For one thing, I have confirmed my belief that *markets are everywhere*. China is still supposed to be a communist country, but even here I have found markets just like those in Europe or America. The goods on sale may be far stranger (and the vendors perhaps less strange: there are few sights more colourful than a stallholder in London's Petticoat Lane market in full cry). But otherwise they are no different – a huge variety of goods and sellers, from which a throng of customers somehow make choices.

Choice defines markets, even in an authoritarian country like China. The girl in the red shirt was not forced to mend my hems; nor was I forced to accept her price. Either of us could have vetoed the bargain – she deciding to wait for another customer and me looking for a repair somewhere else. You can't call something a *market* unless both sides can simply walk away.

> *There are few sights more colourful than a Petticoat Lane stallholder in full cry.*

But we didn't walk away, because there was *mutual benefit* in this exchange. To me, five Yuan was a small sacrifice for the benefit of looking smart. To her, it was a good reward for a few minutes' work. In this way, as we will see in Chapter 2, the market brings about a calm *cooperation* between people who *specialize* in different things that they are good at – she on her skill with a needle, for example, and I on my economics.

Indeed, the greater our *differences* – like my uselessness at sewing and the fact that, on my travels, I lacked the simple *specialist tools* for the job – the easier is it for us to cooperate. We did not need to debate how important my repair was, or have a public vote on whether it should be done. We did not need everyone to agree that the repair would benefit society. In fact it was our very *disagreement* about things – she valued my money more than her time, I valued her skill more than my money – that brought us together. All we had to agree on was price. Beats politics as a way to get things done, doesn't it?

NOBODY'S PERFECT

Markets are human. They're never perfect. If you own an economics textbook, you should rip out the section on 'perfect competition' – the one that describes the perfect balance that prevails in markets when vast numbers of individual producers sell identical goods to vast numbers of individual buyers, all of them completely aware of every price paid in every transaction. That's not 'just a theoretical abstraction' – that's just plain *daft*. As Chapter 2 explains, it's their very *imperfections* and *imbalances* that make markets *work*.

I'm sure there are indeed vast numbers – millions – of individual seamstresses in China. But a stranger like me would have a hard job finding them, never mind comparing them all. As Chapter 3 shows, such *information* is the grit in the market oyster. Information isn't free and perfect. Buyers have to spend time and energy seeking out the sellers they prefer, and sellers have to spend time and energy attracting buyers. If all buyers were perfectly informed, advertising executives would all be out of work. (And we wouldn't want that, would we?)

It's their imperfections and imbalances that make markets **work.**

I too had to spend some effort in looking for someone to do my repair. In my case this *search cost* (as economic jargonauts call it) was pretty minor, but if you were buying something expensive – like a house or a car – you would want to look around more widely, and spend quite a lot of time and care on your selection.

You'd probably want to spend time drawing up a contract, too, just as I had to spend some effort explaining what I wanted and finding out the price. These are called *transaction costs*. Without them, lawyers would be out of work too (but that's life, sadly – things are never perfect).

TIME, PLACE AND TRUST

So I worked on the basis of incomplete information. I knew there was a group of older needlewomen who squatted on a street corner a few blocks away. But I had walked enough, and it didn't seem worth bothering to check them out. Anyway, I had more *trust* in my red-shirted friend: the fact that she could invest in her own little kiosk suggested that the quality of her work attracted a stream of loyal customers.

These differences of *time*, *place* and *trust* (detailed in Chapter 6) all affected my choice. But it's these differences that drive markets. To me, these sellers were *not* identical. There were even differences in the spices on sale in the market, which discerning customers sniffed and tasted, before crossing over to check those on other stalls. Perhaps some were fresher, others cheaper. Or perhaps some stall-holders had a more useful selection.

With such choosy customers, sellers face the constant threat of losing trade to other sellers – which makes them strive to deliver the range, quality and price that people actually want. The *competition* (as Chapter 5 will show) doesn't have to be 'perfect' – having even two similar traders within striking range of each other is enough to keep them sharp. Sometimes the mere *threat* of competition is enough.

WHO? WHAT? WHERE? WHY?

This all means that markets are a continuous voyage of *discovery* for both buyers and sellers. Buyers are constantly tasting the spices, smelling the soup, squeezing the melons, tapping the glassware, checking the prices, and deciding which sellers they trust. Sellers are always adjusting their prices in response to how much customers are prepared to pay, and what competitors are charging. There is nothing static about this: when you see the word 'equilibrium' in your economics textbook, take a marker pen and blot it out.

> **When you see the word 'equilibrium' in your economics textbook, take a marker pen and blot it out.**

Yet the fact that some traders stay in business year upon year suggests that they are doing something right, and that customers are willing to pay for what they produce, rather than just looking, sniffing, tapping and moving on. Somehow, this discovery process matches up *supply* and *demand* – telling sellers what to produce in order to satisfy the constantly changing, and highly personal, demands of their customers.

> **The entrepreneur always searches for change, responds to it, and exploits it as an opportunity.**
>
> **– Management guru Peter F Drucker**

Getting that right demands a bit of flair. You need to guess what buyers might go for, and give it a try. You have to be a bit of an *entrepreneur* – take a chance, invest your time and money in something new that might work, or might not – like those clever cyclists who pedal soup to their customers, or calculate that someone will actually pay hard cash for used cardboard boxes.

UNORGANIZED ORDER

Markets might look like chaotic places – my Lanzhou street market is a river of people, with noise, smoke and clutter – but they are not. There's certainly no central, controlling authority. People here aren't told what to sell or what price to sell it at (a subject for Chapter 4). Rather, they just gather together and hope they are offering attractive goods at attractive prices. The market doesn't succeed because some authority directs it. It succeeds because its participants follow a *set of rules* that have worked for centuries.

Consider *property rights*, for example. The stallholders' goods (or services, like the time and skill of my seamstress) are theirs. My cash is mine. If they succeed in attracting lots of customers, they get to keep the proceeds. If I don't pay, or they swindle me, that breaks the rules. For markets to work, people's property has to be *secure*.

> ### *If I don't pay, or they swindle me, that's against the rules.*

These rules are so natural to us that most everyday transactions don't require legal documents or contracts. They are done on trust. The customers who buy the strange vegetables or the hen's feet in the market simply expect them to be wholesome (well, as wholesome as hen's feet can be): if not, they might demand a refund, or vow never to return to that stallholder again. Likewise, seamstresses trust that when they've handed back your repair, you won't just run off without paying. Those are the rules.

But life isn't perfect. Sometimes, people's property is harmed by what others do. The underwear seller's stock would be devalued, for example, if the smoke and smell from the food stall drifted on to it. And the general human congestion in this narrow street means it can take some time to get to the stall you're looking for. These *externalities* (in the jargon) can be hard to deal with, but as we'll see in Chapter 7, the market often finds ways to do so. In Lanzhou, the food and the clothes sellers seem to have done it simply by making sure that they are some distance apart.

MARKETS ARE A FORCE FOR GOOD

It seems strange that this system – with no overall directing authority, where people come to sell or to buy, purely with their own interests in mind – actually works so well. But it does, precisely because it enables different people with different purposes and opinions to cooperate peacefully, and because it steers resources quickly and efficiently to where people need them.

Certainly, the market has to answer moral concerns (see Chapter 8) such as the fact that it doesn't leave people perfectly equal. My seamstress is much poorer than I am, for example. And yet, thanks to the market system, she and other people in China are catching up fast, their standard of living doubling every five years. The market system is the most powerful anti-poverty device, and the best wealth-creator, on the planet. That is why you find markets (almost) everywhere.

And there are markets in just about everything. In goods (vegetables, spices, cars); in services (plumbers, teachers, cleaners, actors, prostitutes); in housing; and in financial assets like shares and currency. There are even virtual, online markets like eBay, explored in Chapter 9. Indeed, market exchange is so universal that the word *market* has come to cover the whole idea of exchange – not just the place where people stand around trading things (see box).

GETTING RESOURCES TO THEIR BEST USE

On a corner near the street market in Lanzhou is an even stranger market. Men sit around – dark-skinned country people who look older than their years. Some have sledge-hammers beside them; others, spades; still others, pickaxes. A few of them shoulder paint rollers with improbably long handles. Beside each, as they squat playing cards, is a piece of cardboard bearing a short, hand-written commercial for their qualities as labourers. They come to town each morning in the hope that someone will hire them for a few hours or days.

It's an informal *labour market*. They are not selling goods, but their services. They gather here so that anyone who needs workers knows where to find them, and can do

What's in a ~~name~~ market?

What image does the word *market* conjure up in your mind? Perhaps the obvious one is the image of people congregating, maybe on a set day of the week, to buy and sell things such as food or livestock. Or perhaps you think of the actual building where this trade goes on: like England's impressive nineteenth-century corn markets (which still exist, though mostly as entertainment venues).

However *market* has a more abstract meaning too. It suggests the whole economic activity of buying and selling. And the trade in a particular good or service – like *the insurance market* or *the oil market*.

When you offer something for sale you are said to *market* it. The word also covers the particular group of people you want to trade with – as in *the youth market* or *the tourist market*. It also means the *demand* for particular things, with sellers talking about a *thin market* or a *strong market*. And the price of things that are traded, as in *the market was up today*.

Useful word, *market*. Almost as useful as the real thing.

so easily without having to scour the neighbouring villages. Their chosen spot is near to yet another kind of market – a lattice of streets lined with steel sheds from which is sold every conceivable DIY essential – wood, fixings, baths, radiators, air conditioners, pipes, wire, bricks, tiles, windows, drills, spades, light fittings, paint, ladders, locks and more. They know that the customers here may need people to help dig the drains or paint the ceiling. How convenient that there is a labour market nearby!

Convenient, but not coincidental. The free-exchange system has an uncanny power to steer the right resources to the right place at the right time.

But that's the miracle of *markets*.

CHAPTER TWO

How Specialization and Exchange Make Us Rich

MARKETS WEREN'T BORN YESTERDAY

The archaeology of the earliest civilizations shows that markets go back a long way. As does history: markets are mentioned as far back as the Old Testament of the Bible, where Ezekiel writes about brass, oil, honey, wheat and labour being traded in the marketplace; while in the New Testament, Jesus spectacularly disrupts the Temple's lucrative foreign-exchange market.

Tomb paintings show us exactly what markets were like in ancient Egypt. One from Thebes shows a quayside with boatmen exchanging grain for fish and women selling bread and beer. Another shows people trading fish, fruit and cloth. A third shows someone trading a pair of sandals for a cup of sweet drink called *sat*. (Must have been good stuff. Or shoddy sandals.)

This was *barter* – one good was exchanged directly with another. But it's not easy to remember what every good is worth in terms of every other: how much beer can you get for a pair of sandals, say, or how much cloth for a fish? So people started to quote the rate at which they would exchange things in terms of one single commodity. This was the beginning of *money*.

In Egypt, grain served as the standard measure. It wasn't a very durable currency, being hard to protect from pests like mice, insects or tax collectors. Soon, therefore, more durable commodities like gold, silver and copper came to be used.

MONEY MAKES THE WORLD GO ~~ROUND~~ OBLONG

Money made exchange much easier, and then markets really took off. Athens had a very grand marketplace, the *Agora*, near the Acropolis. Today it's a ruin, but 2500 years ago it was hugely busy, with people not just buying food, cloth, slaves and other essentials, but also discussing business, philosophy, culture and politics. Indeed, it's where Athenian democracy was born.

Rome's *Forum* was also more than just a market square (it was actually oblong – the architect, Vitruvius, gave it dimensions of 3:2). It served as a judicial, civic and religious centre, with temples and meeting halls around it and public speaking platforms (*rostra*) within it. Armies would parade through it each time they had humiliated some barbarian nation: the Triumphal Arch of Septimus Severus (AD 203) still stands.

The impressive mediaeval marketplaces of Europe also survive. The largest is in Krakow, Poland, but they are all vast – the suburban shopping malls of their day. Moscow's Red Square seems almost designed for Soviet military parades, but in fact it began life as a marketplace. Markets were big, important and everywhere (at least until the Soviet military parades started).

In England, churches were the social heart of the community: markets would be held near them, often on Sunday, when everyone would be passing by. Goods, news and opinions would be exchanged, workers hired, livestock sold, horses shod and farm tools repaired.

The trade provided rich pickings for kings and manorial lords, who (like the Roman Senate centuries before) controlled the rights to hold markets; and the logistics of getting to market furnished them with a neat rule to beat off the competition from other places. Market day was just that – people would spend up to a third of a day travelling to market, a third doing business, and a third travelling home again. Since people could travel roughly twenty miles in a day, the calculation was that markets must be at least six and two-thirds miles apart. The rule is still used as the basis for market rights today.

The trade provided rich pickings for kings and lords.

As in Greece and Rome, markets and civil administration went together. Many English towns still possess their mediaeval market halls, raised on stone or wooden pillars, where the business of trade went on below, the business of justice and government above. Atop, a bell would ring to start and end the day's trading – a practice that still survives on Wall Street today.

EXCHANGE IS NATURAL

The main business of markets was, and is, *exchange*.

Exchange is so natural that even kids do it without thinking. Ever since the first sandwich was created (probably 2000 years before the Earl of Sandwich claimed the credit), school children have opened their lunch boxes, stared longingly across to the next kid's, and agreed to swap.

They have been swapping toys and trinkets for just as long. Indeed, whole industries have been built on it – from the first cigarette, tea and confectionary trading cards of the 1880s to today's sticker books, where stickers are sold in random packs and the only way to assemble a full set of World Cup players, for example, is to swap your duplicates with someone who has spares of what you want.

But mostly, we don't exchange goods directly, like ancient Egyptians bartering sandals for *sat*. (Just as well, or thirsty shoemakers would be desperate to find ill-shod brewers.) Instead, we make the process of exchange much more convenient and transparent by using *money*. It's called *selling* and *buying*, but it's still just a sophisticated form of exchange. We exchange (*sell*) our own time, skill and products, for cash – cash which we can then use, as and when we choose, to exchange for (*buy*) different goods and services produced by others.

WHY WE EXCHANGE SO MUCH

Everyone on the planet engages in exchange – because everyone gains from it. If your mother has packed three cheese and pickle sandwiches already this week, you yearn for a change – exactly like your friend who has endured three egg and tomato ones. A simple exchange gives each of you something that you prefer over something you have. You both gain from the trade. If you didn't, you wouldn't bother to do it.

That seems obvious: but it is often misunderstood, when money is involved. People tend to think of money as wealth, and so they imagine that the only person to gain from a transaction is the one who gets the money – the seller; while the one who hands over the money – the buyer – inevitably loses.

Governments manage to make paper completely worthless by printing pictures of dead presidents on it.

That's absurd – why should anyone agree to an exchange that leaves them worse off? But until the nineteenth century, the entire international trading system was built on this idea. Countries promoted their exports, and banned or taxed imports, hoping to rake in as much gold and silver as they could and to pay out at little as possible. (A rather pointless pursuit: gold and silver look nice, but once you're weighed down with gold jewellery and your tables are groaning with silver tea sets, all you can do is put this 'wealth' in a vault.)

These days, the situation is even worse, because you don't even get paid in hard metal – just paper. *Blank* paper you could at least write on, but governments manage to make it completely worthless by printing pictures of dead presidents on it. All you can do with this stuff is to pass it on to other people who are willing to accept it in exchange for things that *you* want, in the hope that someone else will in turn accept it in exchange for something that *they* want.

Icelanders, for example, export fish to Germany, getting Euros in return. You can't spend Euros in Iceland: but that's fine, because you can use them to buy BMWs from Germany, wine from France, or fashions from Italy. Cash makes the trades easier, but the principle is just the same as kids swapping stickers: people trade what they have plenty of in return for what they want instead.

Nor is exchange limited to just two partners. A notorious example was the eighteenth-century 'triangular trade'. Caribbean planters sent sugar, cotton, rum, tobacco and coffee to Europe; the same ships took Europe's cloth, guns and hardware to Africa; and there, they loaded up with cargoes of slaves for the Caribbean plantations. Chillingly neat.

COLLABORATION THROUGH . . . DISAGREEMENT

It may seem puzzling that one person can buy, and another person can sell, the same thing for an agreed price, and both think they have done a really great deal. Yet the only reason it puzzles us is because we tend to think that every good has a single, specific *worth* or *value* of its own: surely no sensible person would be willing to pay more, or take less, than that set value?

But *value* isn't set. Value is a personal thing: like beauty, it is in the eye of the beholder – *subjective* rather than *objective*. If we all valued things identically, we would never have cause to exchange anything at all. Trade happens, and is possible, only and precisely because we each value things differently. The kid needing just one sticker to complete a sticker book would gladly give a fistful of others for it. The Icelandic seafarer with plenty of fish in the hold would willingly exchange it for the price of a BMW.

In fact, the *more* that people disagree on the value of things, the *easier* it is for them to collaborate by exchanging them. The difference in their valuations makes it more likely that they will agree a swap, and the more they will each think they have gained from the trade. As a kid I once got a pink hairgrip out of a party cracker: but one of the girls who'd got a water pistol was delighted to swap. I didn't even *try* to swap it with another boy.

Was Manhattan *worth* the price?

Value is *subjective*, a matter for individual judgement. Two people can exchange something, and each congratulate themselves on having got a good deal, precisely because they put different values on the thing that they exchanged.

That's why the native Canarsie people who traded Manhattan Island to the Dutch for $24-worth of glass beads must have thought themselves pretty shrewd. And who is to gainsay them? In 1626 Manhattan was a barren wasteland full of snakes and bloodsuckers. (Some uncharitable people say that nothing much has changed.)

And it's worth remembering that if the Native Americans had invested the $24 at 6% compound interest, today they'd still have enough in the bank to buy the whole place (skyscrapers and all) twice over and have about $1 billion in change.

The ability of the market to promote cooperation, even between people with diverse – indeed opposing – views, is one of its most astounding and attractive features. You might imagine that human beings could cooperate only if they agreed a common purpose, and a common programme for achieving it. But through exchange, they can collaborate and benefit each other, without needing to construct any such political or practical agreement. They do not need to thrash out their differences, nor even be aware of them. They can remain implacably opposed in their view of the world. All they need to know, and agree, is the price at which they are prepared to exchange things.

SPECIALIZATION AND EFFICIENCY

Markets, then, create something positive out of human differences. And they encourage humans to make use of their differences in ways that maximize this creative benefit for us all. They encourage us to *specialize* and then exchange some of what we produce with other people who specialize in producing other things. And we do this because it is very much more effective than trying to make and do everything for ourselves.

In the mid-1970s, the BBC screened a TV comedy called *The Good Life*, in which a couple (played by Richard Briers and Felicity Kendall) decide to quit the rat race and become self-sufficient. The fact that they have to give over their garden to vegetables, chickens and goats causes comic consternation among their smart suburban neighbours; but another comic thread is their discovery that all this self-sufficiency is actually very hard work. Maybe commuting isn't so bad after all.

But why try to do everything yourself anyway? You need different knowledge, skills, land and equipment to raise goats and grow potatoes; and strong fences to keep the first from eating the second. It makes sense for different people to do the two jobs, and to exchange milk and vegetables as they need them. That way, each can become expert, skilled, better-equipped and more efficient, which means that between them, they will be able to produce more than if they each tried to do both jobs.

All this self-sufficiency is actually very hard work.

This system of specialization and exchange – this *market* system – allows human beings to collaborate on a really enormous scale. Nearly every thing we use today comes to us through exchange, rather than by making it for ourselves. And every stage of the manufacture of such things also depends on the specialization and exchange of many people. Adam Smith (see box) recognized this as far back as 1776. Even the most basic product, he explained, involved the work of a 'great multitude' of specialists, all brought together through exchange. A labourer's coarse woollen coat, for example, contained the work of shepherds, carders, dyers, spinners, weavers and fullers. Merely transporting the materials required sailors, ship builders and sail makers. Even their tools depended on:

> *The miner, the builder of the furnace for smelting the ore, the feller of the timber, the burner of the charcoal to be made use of in the smelting-house, the brick-maker, the brick-layer, the workmen who attend the furnace, the mill-wright, the forger, the smith . . .* (Adam Smith, *The Wealth of Nations*, London, 1776)

Hundreds more would be involved in producing the labourer's shirt, shoes, bed, fireplace, kitchen utensils, furniture, tableware and windows. In short, the market system of specialization and exchange gives each of us 'the assistance and cooperation of many thousands'. Without it, we would be a lot poorer.

THE HUGE PRODUCTIVE POWER OF SPECIALIZATION

Without specialization, we would be poorer, because specialization is so much more productive than trying to do everything for ourselves. Smith's famous example is pin making. It seems a 'trifling manufacture', but making a pin is not easy. You need to draw out the wire, straighten it, cut it, sharpen one end and flatten the other to receive the head, which in turn must be made and attached. Then the pins must be whitened and packed . . . .

A wealth of intellect

Adam Smith (1723–1790) was born in the Scottish trading port of Kirkcaldy. Though briefly kidnapped by vagrants as a child, he sailed through school, and became a professor at the University of Glasgow. A book on the psychology of ethics brought him fame, and led to him being hired as personal tutor to a young nobleman. (An odd choice: though brilliant, Smith was notoriously distracted and absent-minded. He once fell into a pit because he was not looking where he was going, and on another occasion brewed bread and butter instead of tea. Not someone you really want to put in charge of your kid.)

While taking his young student around continental Europe (where he met the leading European intellectuals), Smith began writing his great economics book, *The Wealth of Nations* (1776). It took apart the trade barriers, monopolies and commercial restrictions of his day and championed the benefits of free markets and competition. All the leading politicians read it, and it kicked off the great nineteenth-century era of free trade.

In fact, there are about eighteen different steps in making this simple product. You or I, trying to do them all, could probably not make even twenty pins a day, says

Smith – and perhaps not twenty in a year if we had to mine and smelt the metal too. But in a pin factory, the work is divided between specialist workers who do only one or two of the separate operations. Between them, a ten-strong team of skilled pin makers can make 48 000 pins in a day – thousands of times the output of a single person.

That is a huge rise in productivity, in just a 'trifling man-ufacture'. So imagine what huge benefits such specializa-tion could generate across the whole economy. But how can such enormous gains be possible?

SPECIALIZATION MAKES YOU SLICKER

One reason is people's different natural abilities. Even school kids know which of their classmates are the best athletes, the biggest brain-boxes or the neatest writers. Hang out with the football team to look cool, but if you're copying someone's homework, sit next to the class swot.

Hang out with the footballers to look cool, but copy homework off the swot.

Given such natural differences, specialization makes sense. Someone with big strong hands might make a good builder, but a poor watchmaker. A shy person might make a conscientious office clerk, but a bad politician. So the builder who needs a watch repair goes to the neat-fingered specialist; and the office clerk who needs a politician . . . . Well, bad example, but you see the point.

People also *like* doing different things. I like economics, and by specializing, I can spend my life doing what I enjoy. I don't like cooking, but luckily my local Italian restaurateur, Ricky, enjoys every minute of it. So I write books on economics, and spend some of the proceeds at Ricky's restaurant, and everyone's happy.

A third reason is that specialists don't waste time moving between one task and another. Kingsley Amis, author of *Lucky Jim*, once commented that nobody could do creative writing if they had to cook for themselves and wash up afterwards. It may not take long, but it's very distracting. Pop to Ricky's place and you can be thinking up your next line while *he* does the cooking.

Specialists also *hone their skills* through repetition. Ricky can spin pizza dough with amazing deftness, because he does it every day. When I try, it's a mangled mess. And he's skilled at understanding his market too – knowing what his customers want to eat and drink, which suppliers give best value, and where to find reliable staff. If I tried to open a restaurant, I'd be floundering within weeks. It needs expert, local knowledge that can only be gained through experience.

CAPITAL ACCUMULATION

Perhaps the main reason why specialization is so hugely productive is that specialists find it worthwhile to invest in labour-saving tools, machinery and equipment. It's possible to catch fish with your bare hands; but spend a little time making a hook and line, and you can catch more; spend a bit more time making a net, and you can catch more still. Build a boat, and you are really in business. Invest in a diesel-powered boat with sonar, and you're knee-deep in fish.

Of course, no single family eats enough fish to justify that sort of expenditure for themselves. But it makes perfect sense for the specialist seafarer, who catches fish with the intention of exchanging them for something else, since it raises productivity so enormously.

Welcome to capitalism – where instead of consuming everything you produce, you save a little and use it to acquire labour-saving, specialist equipment that enables you to produce even more. In the jargon, you earmark some of your income as *capital*, which you spend on performance enhancing *capital equipment*. And the more capital a community accumulates, the more things it can produce, the more it has to exchange, and the more everyone within it benefits. Today we live in a luxury undreamed of by mediaeval kings, not because we work harder, but simply because we have more capital working for us.

THE SPIRALLING SUCCESS OF SPECIALIZATION

It's a virtuous circle. By specializing, we produce more, generating more wealth. That allows us to spend more on equipment that enables us to produce even more, generating more wealth, which we can use to buy still more labour-saving equipment . . . and so on.

True, the circle depends on us being able to exchange the huge surplus that we produce for things that we actually want more. But that comes quite naturally to human beings. And we lubricate the process even further through inventions like money (which makes exchange much easier) and the capital market (which gives specialist producers access to the performance-enhancing capital they need).

Indeed, it's a growing circle. The usefulness of a telephone network grows massively as more subscribers are added, because the number of possible two-way chat combinations rises geometrically. Likewise, the more specialists that spring up, then the more opportunities there are for exchange, and the more the benefits of the market system accelerate.

Exchange, specialization, and the huge productivity gains that specialization makes possible, are the drivers of our rapid economic progress today. Thanks to them, we have come a long way from the quayside bartering of the ancient Egyptians.

CHAPTER THREE

The Instant Messaging System of Price

Extraordinary scenes of public mourning followed the tragic death of Diana, the former Princess of Wales, in 1997. Nowhere more so than in London, where hundreds of people felt moved to lay floral tributes outside her home, Kensington Palace.

Soon the hundreds had become thousands and the carpet of flowers spread across the adjoining park. Thousands more laid tributes outside Buckingham Palace and against the walls of the Prince of Wales's official residence close by.

London's florists hardly knew what hit them. Their shelves emptied as fast as they could be refilled. But thousands of mourners were still willing to pay top prices to have bouquets to add to the spreading sea of flowers, so they could say that they were a part of this extraordinary event.

The eye-watering price of flowers had an effect closer to home.

It was not just the florists in central London who felt the effects of all this. As florists telephoned their wholesalers to demand new stocks right away, wholesalers found themselves running out also. They could raise their prices, but still the demand kept coming. Now they, too, were desperate.

The world's largest flower market, at Aalsmeer in the Netherlands, had not seen anything like it since Valentine's

Day. And at least they could plan ahead for Valentine's Day. Eyeing the spiralling prices, growers in distant Kenya (which claims to supply a third of the world's flowers) started cutting more blooms and booking more cargo space so that they, too, might benefit from this unexpected surge in demand.

But for me, the eye-watering price of flowers also had an effect closer to home. With my wedding anniversary coming up, Christine would have to make do with a box of chocolates this year, instead of a nice bouquet. And I guess that lots of people with birthdays didn't get much more than a card, while patients in hospital found their visitors bringing grapes instead of gardenias.

PRICE IS AN INSTRUCTION AS WELL AS A FACT

Prices tell us two important things. The first is what things exchange for: how much of one thing you have to give up to get another. The price of a bottle of sweet wine today is however many dollars, or euros, or yen you have to pay for it. To the ancient Egyptian, the price might be simply a pair of sandals. Price is the rate of exchange which people are willing to accept between one good (or service) and another, or between it and money.

That is the rather dull fact that the economics textbooks focus on. (If you have followed my advice and torn out that section, you'll just have to take my word for it.) But prices tell us something much more interesting, more useful, and more important too.

Prices tell us *what to do*. The fact that mourners in London were prepared to pay much higher prices for flowers told florists to order more. Florists' willingness to pay more told the wholesalers to buy more at the market. The higher prices that wholesalers were willing to pay told Kenyan growers to cut more flowers and book more cargo space.

Prices are the instant messaging system of the market.

In other words, the rising price of flowers told everyone in the supply chain what to do. And it told customers like me what to do as well: don't buy flowers unless you're really, really serious about it – send something else instead.

And all this happens at astonishing speed. One day the shop vases are full, the next day florists are screaming orders to their wholesalers, and the day after that, growers in Kenya are booking more cargo space. Prices are the instant messaging system of the market. *Rising* prices show us where things are getting scarce, and where we could profitably invest our time, money and effort to produce more of what will fill that gap. *Falling* prices show us where things are getting more abundant, and prompt us to switch our focus into producing different things that will satisfy people's more urgent needs.

BUYERS, SELLERS AND MARKET PRICES

Prices, of course, depend on people's willingness to pay. And that's limited. In a market, if you want something, you have to give up something else to get it. But it makes no sense to give up more than you have to. After all, anything you save can be used to purchase other things that you also value. That Aston Martin looks nice, but maybe if you bought a cheaper car, you'd have enough left to fix the roof as well.

It depends on your priorities: but generally speaking, the more expensive a thing is, the less people will buy, and the cheaper it is, the more they will buy.

For sellers, it is the exact opposite. They want to make a profit, by charging as much as they can. If the price of something is high, the more they will bring to market in the hope of doing just that. And if the price of something is low, the less they will be willing to sell. If the price doesn't even cover their costs, they won't bother turning up at all.

X MARKS THE (PERFECT) SPOT

This makes life very neat for the textbook writers, who can construct a *demand curve* sloping down (showing that at lower prices, customers demand more), and a *supply curve* pointing up (showing that at higher prices, sellers supply more) as in Figure 3.1. Where they cross marks the *equilibrium* price – the price at which sellers are willing to

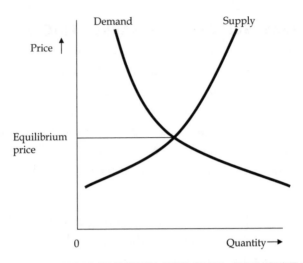

FIG. 3.1 *THE TEXTBOOK 'EQUILIBRIUM PRICE' GRAPH. (NOW YOU'VE SEEN IT, PLEASE TEAR IT OUT, LEST OTHERS SEE IT AND IMAGINE THE WORLD IS REALLY LIKE THIS.)*

sell exactly the amount that buyers are willing to buy. At this price, both sides leave the market happy: buyers fully sated, and sellers precisely sold out.

Sounds good? It gets better. If things work perfectly, the textbooks say, price always gravitates to this happy balance point. If the price were higher, sellers would optimistically bring more goods to market, but would be unable to sell them all, and would have to cut their prices (back to the equilibrium price) to attract more buyers. At a lower price, buyers would be keen to buy, but sellers would be packing up. Buyers would have to offer more (the equilibrium price, in fact) to be sure of getting the goods they wanted. Either way, prices inevitably fall back to the perfect price at which supply and demand are precisely balanced.

NOW THE BAD NEWS

Did that all sound too good to be true? Well it is. In real life, things just don't work like that. People don't always buy more of something just because it's cheap. If someone offered you some really cheap home computers, would you buy them? Probably not: you would be wondering what was wrong with them, and maybe you don't really need more than one home computer, anyway.

Likewise, there was a beer that aimed to attract *more* customers by selling at a *higher* price than its rivals, calling itself 'reassuringly expensive'. And other strange things can happen too (see box). As people get wealthier, for example, they turn their noses up at so-called *inferior goods* (like tripe), even if the price falls – because they can now afford better alternatives (like lean meat).

THE IMPOSSIBILITY OF PERFECT INFORMATION

Nobody said that economics was about real life, but the perfect world of the textbook explanations, where markets always balance, is a strange place indeed. Among other things (for reasons you don't want to know) it depends on

Sell more - raise prices!

The only thing you need to know about economics is that when a thing becomes more expensive, people will buy less of it.

Except sometimes. For example, there are some goods that actually sell more briskly when their price rises. These are called *Giffen goods*.

Sir Robert Giffen was a nineteenth-century Scottish statistician who worked at *The Economist* before eventually becoming head of the Board of Trade. Yet the insight we remember him for today appears nowhere in his many writings. We know it only from an aside in Alfred Marshall's famous *Principles of Economics* (1890). Giffen, he says, observed that a rise in the price of bread was such a big drain on the resources of poor families that they were forced to cut back on their consumption of meat. Since bread was still the cheapest food available, they consumed more of it, even at the higher prices!

there being large numbers of buyers and sellers, who are free to enter or leave the market in an instant, and who can act immediately because they are perfectly informed about who's prepared to buy what at what price.

That's all close enough to the ground of reality to sneak under the barbed wire of common sense: in everyday street markets there are indeed large numbers of buyers and sellers, it's easy to set up a stall and everybody can see who's buying what for how much. But in the wider economy, large companies dominate their markets, newcomers can't build factories in an instant and nobody could know exactly what prices millions of people are paying for the multitude of goods being traded.

> *Nobody said that economics was about real life.*

Indeed, buyers *themselves* don't even know what they will buy and at what price. Often I've been in the supermarket, just happened to spot something that I think would do me well for dinner and have made an impulse buy. And sometimes I just can't believe how much I've paid for a caffeine hit at the station coffee bar, when I'm exhausted and need fortification for the crush home. What we actually buy depends a lot on time, place and whim.

THE MARKET IS A DISCOVERY PROCESS

In other words, life isn't as mechanical as the textbook graphs suggest it is. Nobody could possibly know what millions of consumers like me, with all our whims and foibles, are willing to buy, and at what price. It's not a demand *curve* that sellers face, it's more of a demand *fog*.

How much of something people buy, and at what price, depends entirely on their personal valuation of it (and of the possible alternatives) at that precise *time* and *place*. And people's *valuations* are different: those who buy a stock on Wall Street presumably think it's a good investment, while those who sell it presumably think it isn't. In fact, it's only because people *do* value things differently, and do have different views about what might happen in the future, that markets exist at all.

> *Markets change, tastes change, so the companies and the individuals who choose to compete in those markets must change.*
> **– Computer entrepreneur An Wang**

And those values and expectations *change*. On the death of Diana, people who didn't care much about flowers one day were desperate to get them the next. Meanwhile, others like me, who wanted flowers, decided to change our plans and buy chocolates instead.

In the world marketplace there are millions of people, all buying and selling as their different and changing values, circumstances and expectations take them. Finding your way through such a swirling throng is not simply a case of taking out your textbook graph and seeing where you are.

The market is more of a *discovery process*. If you happen to have the right goods at the right price, place and time, then maybe people will buy. But until you make your pitch, you don't know for sure how strong the demand is, or what the 'right' price might be. You have to take a guess, and learn from the experience of what happens. Entrepreneurs get rich – or go broke – precisely because they are prepared to take such a risk on which products and prices might prove attractive to buyers.

HELP ME, INFORMATION

When you're trying to navigate through a fog, every scrap of information about the landscape is vital. How people get information is crucial to markets – not something that you can ignore, as the textbooks do. Making your way through the market is all about having good information: What might people pay for my new invention? Where can I find a good plumber? Will house prices be cheaper in a year's time? Would I find it easier to get a job if I retrained as something else? Can I buy tomatoes cheaper elsewhere?

And information is definitely *not* perfect. It doesn't grow on trees or float in the air. It's not obvious, nor even objective. The information that you need to navigate through the market exists only in the minds of the individuals who make up that market. It is personal and local. To act on it, you have to *discover* it.

Information is subjective, personal and local.

A property agent, for example, has to know what kinds of property are selling locally, and for what prices. That information changes from *week to week* as local conditions change – a factory closure, say, or a new road being built. A delivery firm needs to know from *day to day* where its vehicles are and where customers want to move goods. A foreign exchange dealer needs to know from *hour to hour* what people will pay for different currencies. A stockbroker may have just *minutes* to act on a tip-off before stock prices move. Information like this drives markets, but there is no possibility that everyone could know it all. By the time the news even reached most of us, it would already be out of date.

THE INSTANT MESSAGING OF PRICE

Luckily, the market has an instant messaging system that tells us all that we really need to know. It tells us where there is scarcity and where there is surplus. It tells us what we need to do to steer our effort towards where it will be best rewarded and away from less urgent uses. This instant messaging system is *price*.

Price isn't some dead fact, the point where two curves on a graph happen to intersect. Price is alive. It's dynamic. It tells us things, and it changes things. When shortages occur – if some tragedy means that there aren't enough flowers in London shops, say – a rising

> **No computer in the world can process information better than the market.**
> **– Former European Commission President Jacques Delors**

price sends the message far and fast (as far as from London to Kenya, in that case, and in just a day or two).

A rising price tells producers all they need to know: that they should produce more, and that customers will thank them for it with high prices. It steers their effort and resources to where they are most needed. And it does so with much more speed and certainty than any central planning authority could muster. If we'd had a Ministry of Flower Supply in 1997, I'm sure it would have been at least a month before anyone even reached for their requisition pad. They probably wouldn't have realized there was a shortage until the weekly or monthly shop returns came in. Then they'd have to analyze the data, calculate the social impact of different strategies, check with other departments. . . .

OUR UNINTENDED GENIUS

So the price system deserves a cheer. It steers resources to their most highly valued uses with speed, accuracy and a minimum of unnecessary detail. It enables millions of people with different – even conflicting – values to benefit each other through exchange.

The price system deserves a cheer.

However, we cannot congratulate ourselves for inventing such an incredibly useful tool. We did not *invent* the price system. We stumbled on it as we went about the entirely natural activity of barter and exchange.

It wasn't our intention to produce the giant instant messaging system that is the price system, nor to make everyone else better off. We traded then for the same reason that we trade now: because we personally benefit from it. In the process, we *do* make others better off, and we *do* create this amazingly efficient information system.

PRICE ELIMINATES WASTE

The price system does not only steer resources to where they are most needed. It also eliminates waste, by prompting producers to find the most cost-effective ways of satisfying customers' requirements.

Builders who need tarpaulins to keep the rain off drying bricks probably don't care whether they are made of traditional tar and jute or today's polyethylene laminates – just as long as they work. But the modern materials are cheaper (and lighter too). Since builders don't want to pay more for waterproofing than they have to, the cheaper modern materials replace the old.

The vast cathedrals of mediaeval Europe were built with scaffolding made of wood. Today, European builders use scaffolding made of aluminium or steel tubes. Go to Asia, however, and you will see people working fifteen or twenty storeys high on scaffolding made of bamboo.

Has someone missed a trick? No. They are each using the cheapest material for the job – the material that has required least effort to produce. Asian builders could use metal poles, but importing them would be expensive. Europeans could use wood, but it would take longer to assemble, and European workers' time is not cheap. Once again, the price system prompts people to favour the most efficient and low-cost way of doing things.

MARKETS ARE ONLY HUMAN

Markets, though, are human. As such, they're never perfect.

Producers, for instance, may misinterpret the price signals, and over- or underestimate what they mean in terms of the demand for their products, leaving them with shortages or surpluses. Or they may recognize what is happening, but be unable to step up their production quickly enough, leaving customers unsatisfied.

Sometimes people just convince themselves that rising prices will carry on rising indefinitely – until the bubble bursts, that is (see box).

The grandly named German field marshal, Helmuth von Moltke the Elder, noted that no battle plan survives contact with the enemy. Nor do producers' plans survive contact with their customers and competitors. Sometimes they can adjust easily – if short skirts go out of fashion,

Tulip mania

Tulips came to Europe in the mid-sixteenth century. In the Netherlands in particular, a garden full of the showy flowers became a powerful status symbol. Competition for bulbs spiralled, as did prices. By the 1620s, a single bulb could cost seven times an average worker's annual salary. By the 1630s, rare varieties went for forty times that. Tulip exchanges sprang up, and ordinary people, eyeing what seemed a certain profit, got in on the mania. People even bought and sold tulip futures.

But by early 1637, prices began to moderate. Profit was no longer a sure thing. Speculators tried to sell their stocks, but fewer people were buying. Certain profit turned into certain loss. In the panic to get out, prices crashed. Within a year, many people were ruined. Some were left holding futures contracts to buy bulbs at prices well above what they now went for in the market.

But some escaped the consequences of their folly: the courts ruled that their debts were the result of gambling rather than business – and so were not legally enforceable.

the same sewing machines can produce long ones instead. Sometimes it's a lot harder. The coal miners thrown out of work by Mrs Thatcher's decision to close down Britain's state-owned pits could theoretically have retrained as hairdressers or interior designers. In reality, mining towns suffered lasting unemployment and decline.

IT'S HARD TO FIND GOOD STUFF

There are other bits of rust on the market mechanism too. Why are the bars and cafés near tourist attractions so awful? One reason is that they don't have to be good because they're convenient: after a day trudging around some museum, the last thing your feet need is another trek to find a restaurant.

Another more important reason is that tourists don't know where the best places are. They might be just a block away, or hidden in a basement right under your nose. If you don't speak the language, it's hard to ask. So you make do with an overpriced, leathery pizza.

If traders are all in one place, everyone benefits.

That's not what a perfect market is supposed to deliver. But your problem is *search costs*. You know what you want – a good pizza – but it takes time and effort to find one. The same is true of people looking for a good plumber or a good mechanic. And that's why we have trade listings in the telephone book, consumer magazines, comparison websites and market analysts. They all exist to give people that information.

It's also why traders come together in markets. English towns have street names like Milk Street, Fish Street and Butcher Row because that's where mediaeval traders collected. I used to think that traders would want to be as far from their competitors as possible. But no: if you're all in one place – a particular street or a particular marketplace – everyone benefits, because customers know exactly where to find you. If they had to check every shop in every street to find what they want, they probably wouldn't bother. When you congregate, you dramatically cut their search costs and make them more likely to come and do business with you.

THE COSTS OF DOING A DEAL

Even when you do find a willing partner, you face other potential burdens – so-called *transaction costs*. You may have to spend a lot of time bargaining before you can strike a deal. Even then, you may fail to agree. If you do agree, you might want a signed contract before you actually hand over the goods or the cash. The sale contract for a large piece of property (or the services of an international soccer star) can run to hundreds of pages, and take thousands of hours of lawyers' time to prepare – which isn't cheap. And then, if one side breaks the agreement, there is the cost of taking action to enforce it.

If search or transaction costs are too high, they can eclipse the gains from an exchange and make it pointless. Some markets (like pensions, for example) are so hard to fathom that many people decide not to bother. Or (like mobile phone and utility contracts) customers stick with an expensive supplier because the effort of finding a cheaper one is too great.

> **Some markets are so hard to fathom that many people decide not to bother.**

I had something of this problem many years ago in New York's Staten Island Ferry terminal. With time to wait, I decided to have a sandwich at its very downmarket greasy-spoon café. Back home in Britain, rail and ferry sandwiches were invariably awful – white bread, curling at the edges, and tasteless fillings. But I decided to brave it, and asked for a cheese sandwich.

The New Yorker behind the bar looked at me as if I was an idiot. 'What kinda cheese you want?' he demanded. 'You want American cheese? You want Swiss cheese? You want . . . ?' He reeled off more. But as I stood there stunned, he went on: 'What kinda bread you want? You want white? You want rye? You want pumpernickel? You want a bagel . . . ?' Before he even exhausted the possibilities, I said I would look at the menu options more carefully and come back in, well, maybe ten minutes, once I'd got to grips with the choice.

CHAPTER FOUR

Killing the Messenger

ZEN AND THE ART OF PRICE MAINTENANCE

My father was a mechanic, and old enough to remember when cars had running boards and starting handles. Some even had little temperature gauges sticking up at the front, above the radiator, to show if the engine was overheating, as engines of the time often did.

One day, a customer came in, worried that each time his car had been running for a few minutes, the temperature gauge would edge up into the red. He thought that the water in his cooling system was about to boil.

My father tested the car, but found nothing wrong: the only fault was that the temperature gauge was over-reading. But the customer remained agitated, and my father knew that telling him simply to ignore it wasn't enough. So, in a move that was certainly no example of motor engineering best practice, he quietly put a blob of solder on the gears of the temperature gauge, such that the needle always came to rest comfortably below the danger zone.

Like a temperature gauge, price reveals the demand hotspots.

The customer was delighted, though I often wonder what might have happened if he had taken his car fully laden up into the nearby hills. He could have had steam pouring out of the radiator, yet have driven on, blissfully content that his engine was running at the perfect temperature.

Fortunately, we heard no more, so I guess this problem did not arise.

Price is like a temperature gauge – it shows us where the hotspots of scarcity are. It doesn't tell us *why* those hotspots occur, any more than the temperature gauge tells us why the engine is overheating. But they both tell us *what to do*. A temperature gauge going into the red tells us to pull over and stop. A rising price tells buyers to use less of the scarce product, and sellers to produce more of it.

SOLDERING UP THE PRICE MECHANISM

Just like a temperature gauge, price works only if you let it. If you solder up the gauge, you won't realize that the car is overheating, and may drive on until you damage your engine. And if you interfere with prices, you won't know where demand is really hottest, and may waste your effort on producing the wrong things.

There are many ways of soldering up the price system. *Governments* can do it through price controls (like minimum wage laws or regulated taxi fares); or by limiting the quantity of things that people are allowed to trade (as with import quotas); or by banning trade entirely (in narcotics, say). And *individuals* can distort prices too, through having a monopoly (where there is only one seller); or monopsony (only one buyer); or through collusion (where suppliers agree to raise prices); or violence (when the Godfather tells you that either your signature or your brains will go on the contract).

In any of these cases, exchange is not purely voluntary (if there's a gun to your head, it's not voluntary at all), so people are forced to accept prices that they would not otherwise agree to. If government limits the price of bread, for example, bakers have to accept the fact, or stay out of the kitchen.

WAGE AND PRICE CONTROLS

When Robert L Schuettinger and I wrote *Forty Centuries of Wage and Price Controls*, we found that official attempts to control prices have a long (and ignoble) history. Around 1760 BC, Hammurabi of Babylon engraved the official prices for nearly everything on pillars of dolomite in the marketplace. (OK, I know that's only thirty-seven and a half centuries, but the title didn't seem so catchy.) Hammurabi's idea was to curb wage and price rises; but even though they were literally carved in stone, people found ways round the controls, and the policy failed.

In AD 284, the Roman emperor Diocletian fixed maximum prices for beef, grain, eggs, clothing and much else, and set down the death penalty for anyone charging more. In this case, the bakers really did stay out of their kitchens: people no longer brought goods to market because they knew they couldn't get a realistic price for them. The result was widespread shortages.

During the American War of Independence (1775–1783), George Washington's army nearly starved to death in the field because of the price controls on food laid down by colonial governments. Pennsylvania, for instance, had imposed controls specifically to keep down the price of goods that the army needed. But once again, nobody bothered growing food for sale when they got scant return for their effort; and unsurprisingly, food became scarce. Only when the controls were repealed in 1778 did the army (and everyone else) at last get enough to eat.

You would think legislators would have got the message.

The French revolutionaries made the same mistake with the 1793 Law of the Maximum, a long list of price controls on grain and other items. Before long, people were collapsing in the street through lack of nourishment. Naturally, the revolutionary leader Robespierre never suffered hunger himself; but he was widely blamed for the crisis and lost his head a few months later.

You would think that legislators would have got the message by now. You can't control prices any more than you can control the weather. You can pass a law saying that every day will be sunny, but don't expect people to come out in their shorts when it's actually snowing. You can pass a price regulation, but don't expect people to bring their produce to market if they know they're going to make a loss on it.

CONTROLS MESS UP THE MARKET

The reason this is important is because prices are not some dead economic statistic. Prices contain real information about the state of supply and demand, and they are the spur to real human action. They tell people where their efforts and resources are most urgently needed, and they give people the incentive – the prospect of profit – to direct their efforts and resources precisely to that hotspot. If prices are not allowed to work, the information and the incentive are lost, and human effort is misdirected.

> *Rent control has destroyed entire sections of sound housing in New York's South Bronx. It has led to decay and abandonment throughout the entire five boroughs of the city.*
>
> *– Walter Block*
> *in The Concise Encyclopaedia of Economics*

A modern example might be *rent controls*. People who rent properties are generally poorer than those who own them; and in the attempt to ensure that poor tenants have affordable places to live, many governments set limits on what rents can be charged.

To see the result, take a trip to the South Bronx. It's reckoned that in the 1970s alone, almost a third of a million New York apartments were simply abandoned, rather than be rented out at a loss by their owners. And the damage continues. When the cost of property loans, repairs and heating continue to rise but rents don't, what is any owner to do? First they might put off redecoration and maintenance. Then they might cut back on services. Eventually, even necessary repairs become unaffordable, and the property starts to crumble. By smothering the price system, we've ended up smothering the market itself.

DISTORTING PRICE THROUGH SUBSIDY

Subsidies are another way of soldering up the price system, with similarly unpleasant and unintended effects. The European Union's Common Agricultural Policy (now gradually being reformed) paid high prices to EU farmers to encourage them to produce foodstuffs – more, indeed, than customers wanted to buy. The result was the much scorned 'butter mountain' and the universally ridiculed 'wine lake'; while millions of tomatoes, which could not be so easily stored, were simply destroyed. Left alone, market prices would have told farmers exactly how much food customers wanted: but the higher subsidized prices prompted them to produce a surplus.

Such overproduction was a clear example of effort and resources being wasted when government subsidies overrule the price system. But subsidies can make *buyers* do wasteful things too. When the price of bread was heavily subsidized in Hungary (to make it cheaper for consumers), enterprising builders bought it to use, not as food, but as a building material.

And smothering the price system in one market can also have perverse effects in others. In 2006, America's biofuel producers were handed billion-dollar subsidies as part of Congress's efforts to promote 'green' energy. The flood of cash allowed them to buy up vast quantities of corn, which then shot up in price. Consequently there were riots in Mexico, where corn is a particularly important part of the diet, especially of poorer people.

Subsidy distorts markets because it gives both producers and consumers wrong information about where the demand hotspots really are. And *taxes* do the same thing. In an attempt to encourage people to buy recycled building material rather than dig fresh gravel out of the ground, Britain imposed a tax on the digging, called the Aggregates Levy. But by raising the price of gravel, the tax encouraged illegal quarrying, which became a very profitable business, especially for certain criminal elements.

THAT OL' BLACK MARKET

Nothing helps the criminals, though, more than an outright *ban* on some market. Between 1920 and 1933, America banned the manufacture, transportation and sale of alcohol – Prohibition. The ban did not end the demand for alcohol, of course, particularly since much of the population enjoyed a drink, regarded it as harmless and resented being criminalized. So a vigorous black market grew up, with Americans enjoying cocktails (designed to disguise the taste of the rough liquor) in illegal speakeasies, courtesy of the Mafia (who were perhaps the only folk to benefit from the legislation).

In 1937, New York adopted another bizarre measure, the Haas Act, which stopped any new taxicab licences being issued. Over the next few years, the number of cabs, which had peaked at 21 000 in 1931 (taking drinkers home from the speakeasies was good business), fell to 11 878 as drivers left the trade (the Depression was definitely *not* good for business). It remains at that number. Today's demand for taxis in New York warrants a much bigger supply, but the ban still stands. If you want to go into the taxi business you have to buy your 'medallion' from an existing driver, at a price now in the hundreds of thousands of dollars. That's why New York taxis are so darned *expensive*: there aren't enough of them.

> ### That's why New York taxis are so darned expensive.

Wartime *rationing* (which the British government only got round to abandoning completely in 1954) had a similar effect. So-called black markets, which were in fact *real* markets breaking out from the controls, were all around. Everything could be bought, and in any quantity – at a price. But since these markets were illegal, the sellers were

> *There is no way in which one can buck the market.*
> **– Prime Minister Margaret Thatcher to the House of Commons, 1988**

often less than reputable: the 'wide boys' (so named from the extravagant cut of their lapels) charged high prices to compensate for the risks they were taking.

Black markets still exist in several sectors that are classed as illegal – narcotics, for example. Human exchange is so basic that it seems impossible to stamp it out. Sometimes, as with drugs, the attempt to do so is arguably worse than the problem that provoked the ban.

Quotas are another policy that prevents prices from functioning. When the United States imposed limits on how much steel could be imported, the idea was to protect domestic steelmakers from cheaper steel coming in from abroad. But it also meant that domestic carmakers no longer had access to all this cheaper (and often, better quality) imported steel, and car prices rose.

As well as subsidizing its own farmers, the European Union tries to keep out other countries' *manufactures* too. Limits on the number of undergarments that could be brought in from China prompted the 2005 'Bra Wars' and forced European consumers to pay more for their smalls. Frédéric Bastiat's 1845 spoof petition, in which candle makers complain of competition from a foreign power – the Sun – wasn't so far from reality.

INFLATION

Another thing that smothers the price system is *inflation*. This is when politicians are so careless with our money that it loses its value, and you have to give up more of it to buy almost anything: in other words, when prices rise all over the place. It can reach quite amazing proportions, as with the great German inflation of the 1920s, when people literally burned money – it kept the stove alight much longer than the amount of firewood you could buy with it.

Burn money – it's cheaper than firewood.

However, when prices are rising all around, it's hard to see what the price system is actually telling us. Normally, you would expect to see some prices rising – indicating scarcity hotspots where buyers are prepared to pay handsomely to get what they are short of – and others falling – indicating surpluses. Those would be clear signals for people to switch their efforts and resources to where the scarcity is, and away from the areas that are overprovided. When *all* prices are rising, though, the signal is much less clear. In scarcity hotspots, prices will rise quicker than average, and where there is surplus they will rise less quickly. But that is harder to see: the *signal* of scarcity or surplus is lost amid the *noise* of prices rising all over the place. People's effort is not drawn so quickly and efficiently to where it is really needed. Inevitably, inflation wastes resources.

I GET HIGH PRICES (WITH A LITTLE HELP FROM THE STATE)

Private agencies can distort markets too. One example is *monopoly*, the situation where there is only one seller of a particular good or service. That is always bad news for buyers. If there are no other suppliers that they could go to in search of a better deal, the monopoly can charge pretty well what it likes.

Yet in the market economy, monopolies are actually pretty rare, and seldom exist without some kind of state regulation to protect them. Even a private mine that is the sole source of some particular mineral can't take its customers for granted. If it charges too much, they may simply stop using its product; or they might switch to something less good that still does the job; and its high charges encourage entrepreneurs to look for some new source of supply, or to invent new substitutes.

There is even less chance of holding on to a dominant market position if you are only a retailer, or a media group, or a carmaker. Big as you might be, it's always possible that other people, sniffing your profits, could come in and set up in competition to you.

The idea was too good not to abuse.

That's why most monopolies exist among state producers or in markets where state regulation keeps out competitors. In many countries, the government runs postal services, barring competition by law. State bus, rail, water, electricity and gas monopolies are common. Some Nordic states have monopolies on the sale of alcohol (which must be fabulous for their finance ministers). Since the 1980s, there have been worldwide moves to privatize many such industries; but quite often this means creating a few regulated private monopolies, rather than opening things to competition.

Florence was the first modern government to think of granting exclusive monopolies. The architect Brunelleschi got one in 1421, for a boat equipped with gear to lift marble. Then Venice made a system of it, giving ten-year monopolies to inventors, with a penalty of 100 ducats on anyone breaking them.

The idea was too good not to abuse. There may well be a good case for protecting new inventions, but by the 1600s, European kings were giving (or rather *selling*) their chums monopolies on all sorts of everyday items, such as salt, soap, coal and even playing cards – goods that in consequence soared in price and became not quite so everyday any more.

PATENTS AND COPYRIGHT

Official, though temporary, monopolies still exist today in the form of *patents*. They are intended to give inventors time to exploit their brainwave and earn some return on it, protected from imitation by the force of law. The aim is to give people an incentive to invest their time, money and effort in devising new inventions, without imitators immediately copying their ideas and making the profit from them. Patents are particularly important in sectors such as pharmaceuticals, where the development of new medicines can take several years and cost many millions of dollars; but they mean that pharmaceutical companies can charge handsomely for their products.

Unless they face a *monopsony*, of course. That is the situation where there is just a single buyer – and again it rarely happens unless the state is involved. Where state-run healthcare systems, such as Britain's National Health Service, dominate the market, they have the power to force suppliers to accept lower prices. That is nice for taxpayers, at least until the suppliers give up and go to some other country where they can get a better deal.

Copyright is a kind of monopoly granted over communications media such as books, movies, music and so on. In most countries, it persists for 50 or 70 years after the death of the author, whose heirs benefit from the higher prices that the monopoly allows them to charge for the output. You can see the effect in the bookshops when an author's 50 or 70 years are up: all at once there is a selection of new editions, which might be a half or quarter of the price of the same material when it was under copyright.

OCCUPATIONAL LICENSURE: THEN . . .

Back in 1776, Adam Smith in *The Wealth of Nations* famously observed that 'People of the same trade seldom meet together, even for merriment and diversion, but the conversation ends in a conspiracy against the public, or in some contrivance to raise prices.' Well, he was an academic, so he should know about that.

But professional groups have been conspiring and contriving since Roman times and before. By the Early Middle Ages, craftspeople got together, threw some gold into a welfare pot – forming a 'guild' – and agreed to support each other in promoting their sector. (By all accounts the merriment and diversion were pretty good too.) Carpenters, stonecutters, merchants, goldsmiths, cutlers, glaziers, tailors, leatherworkers, butchers, bakers and even candle makers got in on the act, and by the 1300s and 1400s the guilds had become both rich and powerful, and were building dazzling halls for themselves in market squares across Europe.

It's certainly possible to raise prices, for a while at least, by getting together with other people 'of the same trade' and agreeing to keep prices high. There's always the threat that some of your colleagues might cheat on the deal and undercut you, but you can probably make life pretty unpleasant for them. Your real problem is people from other places (or from other professions) spying your vast profits and muscling in. That's the market, though. So to keep your prices high, you have to stop the market from working and limit the competition. For that you need the power of the *state*.

The medical profession is the most powerful mediaeval-style guild in America.

Thus the guilds – arguing that the public must be protected from incompetent workers – sponsored public regulations to make apprenticeships long (six or seven years was common) and scarce (Smith noted bylaws denying Sheffield cutlers more than one apprentice, or Norfolk weavers and English hatters more than two). Even experienced linen weavers could not transfer their skill over to silk weaving without serving a long apprenticeship. Other laws forbade carpenters and builders from one town setting up business in another. It was all 'a contrivance to raise prices' by limiting the supply of potential competitors, and all justified on the grounds of 'public interest'.

. . . AND NOW

What's truly remarkable is that exactly the same still happens today. Why is American healthcare so expensive? Because the medical profession is the most powerful mediaeval-style guild in America. To practise medicine, you need a licence from the state, and to be a graduate of an approved medical school. But it's the profession itself that approves the schools and ultimately decides how many people will be admitted. By making medical training long and arduous, the profession discourages many students from even bothering to apply in the first place. So the number of potential competitors is limited, and fees soar. The cutlers and hatters would have been proud of them.

Yet it's not even clear that any of this actually raises standards. The restricted supply of doctors means that some patient demand goes unsatisfied. People may go untreated, or may turn to alternative therapists with no meaningful qualifications at all. Meanwhile, very able and experienced healers who do not fit the licensing criteria cannot legally practise. Those who do get through will be trained in the orthodox way of doing things: innovation won't be encouraged.

Any one of these measures, whether it be registration, certification, or licensure, almost inevitably becomes a tool in the hands of a special producer group to obtain a monopoly position at the expense of the rest of the public.
– Milton & Rose Friedman in *Capitalism and Freedom*

Britain's lawyers are every bit as good as American doctors at keeping out the competition, and their archaic practices (and dress) are testament to this same orthodoxy and lack of innovation. Getting in is equally difficult – and expensive. To argue cases in the major courts, you need to be a barrister. To be a barrister you need a good law degree and you have to join one of four Inns of Court and turn up to twelve qualifying sessions (formerly known as 'eating dinners'). Then you need to find chambers that will take you as a pupil, but (of course) there are far fewer of those slots available than there are applicants. The lawyers say that this intense (and expensive) training gives the public a Rolls-Royce court service. But how many people can afford a Rolls-Royce?

Which brings us back to the motor trade. Restrictions on supply such as price controls, tariffs, rationing, regulated monopolies and professional licensure all need the power of the authorities to stick. No doubt the governments who promote them do so for the best of intentions, at least sometimes. But when you do not allow the market to work, and solder up the price mechanism, you lose its amazing ability to direct effort and resources to where they are needed, and to eliminate waste. That is why you need, not regulation, but *competition*.

CHAPTER FIVE

The Driving Force of Competition

KEEPING IT IN THE FAMILY

When it comes to eliminating the competition, the Mafia beats lawyers and doctors hands down. Those guys *really* eliminate the competition. I mean *really*. In Sicily, the Mafia's spiritual home, around eighty per cent of businesses cough up protection money; and many of Italy's largest companies do too, not to mention thousands of small ones. That's why the Mafia has grown to become the country's biggest business, accounting for around seven per cent of Italy's economy.

Their trade is booming in other parts of the world too, though these days it's not just drugs, gambling and prostitution. Organized crime is now involved in almost every sector, from textiles to tourism, real estate to finance, service industries to public works and construction. Nor is protection money paid over in used banknotes anymore. They're much more subtle than that. They just come into your restaurant and suggest you use their laundry service for your tablecloths and their bakery for your bread. Sure, it costs rather more, but then you can be sure that there won't be any nasty incidents that will scare away your customers.

THE JOY OF VOLUNTARY EXCHANGE

Transactions based on violence aren't *market* transactions, though. They are plain coercion. Markets are about *voluntary* exchange, where both sides are free to walk away from the deal – and without any threat of retribution. When a pen is placed in your hand and a gun is put to your head, it may well be an offer you can't refuse, but it is not an offer that you *voluntarily* accept.

The joy of *voluntary* exchange is that both sides benefit, not just those who have guns. People accept a voluntary exchange precisely because they get something out of it, not because they are forced to accept it.

> ### *The joy of voluntary exchange is that both sides benefit.*

To repeat: every voluntary exchange, every market trade, makes both parties to it better off: they wouldn't do it, otherwise. In every market transaction, two people are getting some personal benefit, and spreading benefit to the other. And with millions of people all engaging in millions of transactions every day, it's surprising how quickly and how widely that these benefits can spread.

In school I was set a mathematics problem. Ten diners sit round a table, but don't like the people they're sitting next to. So they swap places. But they don't like that arrangement either. It takes just a minute to swap round. How long would it take them to try out every possible seating plan?

The answer is roughly seven years, which shows how many permutations are possible when people do things together. And with billions of people in the world, all exchanging things with each other every single day and in countless permutations, it also shows how the benefits of voluntary exchange can zip quickly around the world.

COMPETITION SPEEDS THE BENEFIT

The more free that exchange is, the faster and further the benefits of exchange can spread. People are much more likely to enter into exchange voluntarily than if they have a gun to their head. People actively seek out potential customers: they don't actively seek out extortionists.

People are also more willing to trade if they have a choice of where, when, with whom and at what price they exchange, because then they are more likely to find exactly what they want. The *wider* the market is – the more potential customers and suppliers that exist – then the more possible permutations there are between potential traders, the more exchange occurs and the wider the benefits of trade spread.

To get the most out of the market, then, people need to be free to trade, or not, as they choose. They need to be able to check the price from one supplier, and move on to another if they think they can get a better deal. They need a choice of suppliers. They need *competition*.

And so do sellers. They need to be able to reject the price offered by a customer, in the hope that other customers will soon come along. There needs to be *competition* on both sides.

And there *is* competition among buyers just as much as there is between sellers. Carmakers bid against each other for steel, and against engineers who want the same steel to make bridges, or even cutlers who want it to make spoons. The outcome will depend on how urgent these competing demands are: perhaps the engineer has no option but to use steel, while the cutler is willing to switch to other metals if the price rises too high.

Competition is the great enemy of waste and indolence.

When competition prevails, prices reflect customers' valuations of things more accurately. Customers are not *forced* to pay more than they think something is worth to them just because there is no other source of supply. Nor are sellers *forced* to take less than they think their goods are worth. Competition brings prices more into line with people's real values. And that means that resources are more accurately drawn to where people really value them.

It also means that those resources will reach their destination more quickly. Competition makes it more urgent for people to act on price signals. When you face competition, you can't afford to wait around while some more nimble person gets the right goods to the right place and steals your customers and your profit. Nor, in a competitive market, can you run an inefficient, high-cost business and stay solvent for very long. Competition is the great enemy of waste and indolence.

COMPETITION ON QUALITY

Competition is not just about price: it's about quality, too. You can charge the same price as someone else, but if your goods or services are better quality, you're offering a better deal, and you will win customers from your competitors.

This *non-price competition*, as it's called, is particularly important in markets where prices are fixed, such as when there are government regulations on what utilities, telephone companies, taxis or airlines can charge. Providers can still compete by offering a quicker or smarter service, greater comfort, wider choices or other features.

Actually this form of competition is more common than we suppose. Across from Scotland Yard in London is a street market in which there are two fruit sellers. (To please their customers, they sell fruit in pounds and ounces, under the very shadow of the police headquarters, even though the law insists they use the metric system. Isn't competition wonderful?) Their prices are always nearly identical, since if one charged much more, customers would simply walk on to the other. So when I buy fruit there, it's on the basis of *quality* – which seller's fruit seems riper or fresher that day. And not just the quality of the fruit: I tend to prefer one fruit seller because I find him cheerier and more help-ful. I decide on the basis of *service*.

Hobson's (lack of) choice

Thomas Hobson (1544–1630) was an enterprising carrier in Cambridge, England, who rented out his spare horses to students and staff of the university. In order to ensure that no horse would be overworked, he operated a strict rotation system. Prospective clients were told they could have the next horse in the rota-tion order, or none at all – a policy that came to be known as 'Hobson's choice'.

It's the fear that customers can go somewhere else that keeps traders on their toes, and pushes them to provide customers with the quality they demand at prices they are prepared to pay. That in turn makes suppliers focus on their own cost-effectiveness, putting in stricter cost con-trols and better quality assurance. And it prompts them to demand the same of their suppliers, who then also have to ensure that their operation delivers quality at low cost. In this way, competition focuses the whole economy in delivering good value.

WHY PRICES AREN'T UNIFORM

Competition, then, pressures traders, like my London fruit sellers, to try to match other people's offering in terms of quality and price. So why, in the real world, do you see the same thing for sale at different prices?

One reason is transport costs. Oranges cost more in Scotland than in Cyprus because they have further to travel, and travel isn't cheap. (Cafés in Cyprus often give you the most delicious oranges, free of charge: plainly, transport and distribution are most of what the Scots are paying for.)

Convenience counts for a lot, too. The local store that opens 24 hours a day charges more than the out-of-town supermarket. But if you just need a bottle of milk and don't want to travel too far, or you need some aspirins late at night, you're happy to pay.

Convenience counts for a lot, too.

The price of labour isn't uniform, either. Those shop assistants who work unsociable hours in the local store are better paid than those on the day shift. Some people are paid more because their skills (footballers) or the trust demanded of them (lawyers) are in short supply: which explains why neither football matches nor lawsuits are particularly cheap. Other professions (airline pilots, for example) require long and costly training, which is passed on to their employers in the form of higher wages. And others (oilrig workers, say) demand higher wages to compensate for the risk and danger that they face.

IMPERFECT INFORMATION AND PRICES

But a key reason why prices vary is *information* – or rather, the lack of it. Markets are dynamic, in constant flux. When market conditions are changing rapidly, it's not always easy to find out exactly what is going on.

Every day, customers are moving between suppliers, checking the price and quality of what each has to offer. Every day, some sellers come up with better or cheaper products, forcing their competitors to try to match their offer in order to retain customers. Scientific breakthroughs, changes in the weather, fashion, accidents, health scares, even public funerals, all prompt customers to demand new products and reject old ones. Hotspots of scarcity are always bursting out, first here, then there.

> *Hotspots of scarcity burst out, first here, then there.*

Sometimes, though, prices may be slow to adjust. Perhaps florists think that a sudden rush to buy flowers is only temporary and do not immediately respond by charging more; perhaps they feel that raising prices too much might damage their relationship with their existing customers. And even if prices do rise when there is a shortage, many potential suppliers might not notice it, or might not act upon it. They may be too distant to understand the local situation, for example; or maybe they are not competitive enough to respond; or perhaps it might take time for them to tool up and supply whatever is scarce.

HOW SPECULATORS BENEFIT SOCIETY

So in the melee of the market, pockets of scarcity can co-exist with low prices, and pockets of shortage can coexist with high prices. Indeed, the same item can be scarce in one place and in surplus in another. For a while at least: this situation cannot last too long, any more than one half of a room can remain hot while the other is cold.

The quicker that price differences are eliminated the better, of course. We want human resources to be directed efficiently and quickly towards the hotspots of scarcity, not wasted on serving less urgent needs. And helping this to happen are those superconductors of the market, for whom we should raise another politically incorrect cheer – the *speculators*.

> **Some people think that speculators are**
> **unproductive – but it's not money for nothing.**

Speculators buy when they think that other people have not yet realized that something is scarce (or will become so). They make a guess that prices will eventually rise, and that they will have got a bargain: they can then sell what they bought at a higher price. Or if they think that there's an unrecognized surplus and that prices will fall, they can agree to supply something in the future, but at today's price. And sometimes, if they discover that the price of something is high in one place but low in another, they can buy low and sell high and make an instant profit. This is known as *arbitrage*.

Some people think that because speculators just exploit price movements and don't produce any physical goods, they are unproductive. But it's not money for nothing. Speculators take a risk on future price movements, chancing that their guess about the future is better than other people's. If it isn't, they will lose money. And arbitrageurs have to work at having better information about prices than other people, and to move quickly to take advantage of it before the news spreads.

In either case, though, their actions force prices to react and draw resources more swiftly to where they are most valued. Isn't that worth a cheer?

WHY MARKETS NEED ENTREPRENEURS

Another underestimated group is the *entrepreneurs*. They also smooth out the gaps in the market, not by exploiting price differences, but by producing new goods or services to fill the holes in demand. As the market ebbs and flows, swirls and eddies, they too have to be alert to what opportunities may

Amateurs focus on rewards. Professionals focus on risk.

– Online trading expert Harald Anderson

open up. But their skill is to anticipate whether people will be attracted to a better or cheaper product, or maybe to some completely new one.

Entrepreneurs also take a risk on their predictions of the future. They invest time, money and effort on creating

---

The market is a harsh mistress

In 1957, Ford stoked up rumours that it was introducing an entirely new kind of car. In the event, the 1958 Ford Edsel did not live up to its hype. It borrowed heavily from existing Ford models, and while it did have some new features, they made it more expensive than most people were willing to pay. Meanwhile, the United States was entering a recession, and buyers were looking for less expensive, more fuel-efficient cars. The Edsel flopped – one of the industry's most magnificent failures.

In Britain, meanwhile, Strand cigarettes launched a 1959 advertising campaign with the slogan *You're never alone with a Strand*. It featured actor Terence Brooks lighting a cigarette on a dark, deserted London street. The ad, with its haunting music, won awards. But it didn't sell the cigarettes: buying Strand suggested to people that you were a friendless failure. The brand soon went out of production.

---

something new, and bringing it to market. And crucially, they have to take a *guess* about what price they can charge. They cannot just check on some graph how much of a new product they will sell at each particular price. They have to *discover* it by pitching a price, and seeing what happens. If they get it right, they can make a fortune; wrong, and they can just as easily lose one.

Actually, we are all entrepreneurs. We may not invent some revolutionary product, nor build a new shopping development. But as employees, we scan the labour market and try to spot places where we might be better rewarded, perhaps risking time and money on retraining. Or we may set up a small business, even from home or online, and try to attract customers with our particular mix of service and price.

It's a constant process of trial and error, trying to find where best to apply our effort in a world of constant change. Competition from others makes it all the more urgent.

CREATIVE DESTRUCTION

The economist Joseph Schumpeter called this process *creative destruction*. And true, competition does force some people to abandon their plans and find some other line of business. But it's not destructive in the way that a war is destructive. Nobody gets killed. The aim isn't even to injure other people, just to outpace them, with better market information, or with more attractive products and services.

It's certainly creative, though. As people look for cheaper and better products and processes, it encourages innovation. It prompts people to take risks in identifying and satisfying pockets of demand. And it produces a constant improvement in the goods and services we use: sophisticated items, like today's cars and aircraft, could not exist without innovation and refinement over long periods, driven by competition.

Sometimes the mere smell of competition is enough.

How much competition is needed to achieve this creative result? Sometimes the mere smell of it is enough. Your firm might dominate today's market, but if it's possible for others to assemble enough capital and expertise to take you on, you're unwise to exploit your position, because your high profits will attract competitors. A *contestable* market keeps suppliers sharp, even if, right now, their dominance is not *actually* contested.

In my London street market, the presence of just two fruit sellers seems quite enough. They offer better quality, wider choice and keener prices than the lone fruit sellers on street corners nearby who face no immediate competition. True, the customers of these corner traders could walk a few hundred paces and enjoy the benefits of competitive supply. But enough of them don't bother. Whoever said markets were perfect?

PERFECT NONSENSE

This is all very far from the textbook ideal, with its uniform prices, identical products and perfect information. But it's the very fact that prices go wrong, that information is patchy, that there is profit to be made from fleeting opportunities, which drives the market process. In real markets there is no equilibrium, no stability. It's like trying to rake level the desert dunes when the wind keeps whipping up the sand.

Some people think that competition is wasteful, because production processes must be duplicated. But without the spur of competition, monopoly providers would face no pressure to minimize costs and prices, or maximize choice and quality. They would have no reason to bother finding out what customers really wanted, or taking risks to supply it. Innovation and improvement would both suffer.

> *Competition isn't wasteful – competition is absolutely essential.*

Perhaps the reason why some people think you can do away with competition is that the textbooks assume away everything that is important about it. Their 'perfect competition' denies everything that gives competition life: the fact that producers are different and want their products to be different too; that customers have different values; and the differences in time, place and information that produce the ebbs, flows and surges that motivate human action and spur human progress.

Competition isn't wasteful – competition is absolutely *essential*.

CHAPTER SIX

The Rules of the Market

HONESTY REALLY *IS* THE BEST POLICY

I financed my PhD at the University of St Andrews by restoring and selling antique prints and maps of Scotland. One of my best customers was a Mr Wildman, who ran a smart little antique shop in Edinburgh's Hanover Street. He liked to have my inexpensive local views on display because they attracted passers-by into the shop, where he hoped their eye might fall on one of his *much* pricier pieces of antique furniture.

One day I went in with a very large framed view of Edinburgh, which I knew from its original binding to be over a hundred years old. Yet it was as clean and crisp as if it had been printed yesterday. Mr Wildman seemed suspicious. 'It looks too good to be true,' he said, motioning to decline it. But I really didn't want to carry this heavy, awkward picture back home. I had no proof on me, but I assured him that it really was an antique, and eventually he agreed to take it.

> *Most market transactions are done on the basis of trust.*

Our conversation showed Mr Wildman's professionalism: he did not want to sell his customers a fake, nor have them telling others that he had done so. But his reluctance was also something perfectly natural to us all. Before we give up our money (or labour, or goods) in an exchange, we want to be sure that what we will get in return really is what is promised. If you're buying an antique, you want to know that it is genuine; if you're buying a television or a car, you want some assurance that it will work reliably once you get it home.

If a large amount of money is at stake, you might demand a written guarantee or contract. But most market transactions, like mine with Mr Wildman, are done on the basis of *trust*. He knew me, because we had dealt often before. He knew that I understood my business. And we both knew that if I sold him a fake picture – or for that matter, if he gave me a dud cheque – it would end the trust that made possible our mutually beneficial exchanges. That was reason enough for us both to stay honest.

EXCHANGE IS BUILT ON TRUST

Some people imagine that markets are ruled by *caveat emptor* – let the buyer beware. Certainly, it's wise to inspect the goods before you hand over your cash. But no market could function if buyers believed that sellers were always trying to cheat them. They would spend too long checking out the merchandise, and often there would be no way they could know for certain that what they were being sold was fit for purpose. You can't tell whether you've bought bad eggs until you crack them open; and few of us know enough about cars or televisions to predict how reliable they will be, or enough about medicine to judge our doctor's competence. *Caveat emptor* may be sensible advice, but it can't be the foundation of a thriving market. Markets demand honesty. Markets require *trust*.

Trust comes naturally when you know whom you are dealing with, and deal with them often. I trust my local grocer not to sell me bad eggs because I go there nearly every day: they know me, and they want me to keep coming back. But how can you trust someone you don't know, or deal with only rarely? I don't buy a new car or a new television very often: I don't know the sales staff, and they probably don't expect to see me ever again. So how can I be sure they won't cheat me?

> *The purest treasure mortal times afford, is spotless reputation . . .*
> – **William Shakespeare,** *Richard II*

Actually, it's easy. The market has evolved many ways of gauging the trustworthiness even of people we don't know. Like *reputation*. A local grocery whose goods are always fresh, a car dealer who always fixes faults, a sympathetic and careful doctor, will all build up a good name. Potential customers have only to ask around to discover who delivers good value, or bad.

BRANDS COMMUNICATE TRUST

Such word-of-mouth reputation might work well locally, where there are only a small number of providers, and customers deal with them face to face. But what about the wider, global economy where choice is vast, and the providers may be on the other side of the world?

In fact, even here the market (with a little help from the law) has developed solutions.

One of these is *brands* – names or logos that distinguish one supplier's product from all others, and which cannot legally be used by competitors.

A brand tells customers what to expect. Wherever you are in the world, go to the Ritz and you know you'll get fine food, excellent service and comfort – at a price. Go to McDonalds and you know you'll get low cost, value and speed. Go to a restaurant you've never heard of and you don't know what you'll get.

Brands reassure customers about the quality of what they are buying. That reassurance attracts customers, making strong brands a very valuable asset for producers. When Rolls-Royce was sold in the late 1990s, BMW paid £40 million – not for its car plants, but just for its name, logo, radiator design and Spirit of Ecstasy mascot.

A brand tells customers what to expect.

Allowing your brand to be compromised, either by your own folly or by others abusing it, undermines customers' trust, and can be fatal for business. That is why firms go to enormous lengths to protect strong brands. Coca-Cola retains fleets of lawyers to protect its 'Coke' trademark. In

New Zealand a small country business run by a family called Harrod was sued by the eponymous London department store. McDonald's took legal action against a Scottish café owner of the same name.

LONGEVITY, SOLIDITY AND ENDORSEMENT

Another way to convince customers that you are trustworthy is to point to your *longevity* in business. A firm that sold shoddy goods would soon lose customers and go out of business, but the fact that you have been going a long time tells people that your customers keep coming back. When Harrods proclaims that it was founded in 1834, or Bloomingdales in 1872, they are telling the world that people trust them and keep coming back to them.

And why do firms that rely heavily on customers' trust – banks, lawyers and accountants, for example – build themselves such grand office blocks? Because it proclaims their *solidity*. Only someone who intends to be around a long time would make such a large investment, which tells customers that the firm is confident that it provides an enduringly good service. And the impressive certificates on the walls of those plush offices show the *qualifications* of their professional staff, providing another demonstration to customers of their dedication (all those years of training) and competence.

Advertising is another method. These days, advertising must be truthful, so an advertising message tells customers some essential fact about the product – that it washes whiter, lasts longer, or is cheaper than its competitors. And *celebrity endorsements* show that someone famous trusts your product enough to stake their own precious reputation – their own valuable brand – on its reliability.

IN GOD WE TRUST – OTHERS PAY CASH

Newspaper reports and articles in *consumer magazines* also provide potential customers with information about the reliability of firms and their products. Indeed, consumer magazines make their own reputation out of rating other businesses. So do the specialist *analysts* and *research firms* who sell their findings to customers and investors – a growing sector in a globalized economy where people may be very distant from the firms they buy from or invest in.

Sellers too use specialist *credit rating agencies* to gauge whether their customers can be trusted to pay for the goods or services they order, once the bill arrives. The *reputation* of customers, their apparent *solidity* and *trade information* from other sellers can also help sellers form a judgement.

Cash on the nail.

But if you really want to make sure you are paid, the best thing is to insist, as the merchants of Bristol, England, once did, on *cash on the nail* – the 'nails' being the flat-topped brass bollards outside the city's Exchange building.

SETTING AND ENFORCING THE RULES

Trust, then, is central to markets. Markets aren't dog-eat-dog battles. We are social creatures, and markets are social arrangements. They only work if we respect certain standards or rules of behaviour toward one another. If you want to reap the rewards of friendship, you have to treat friends fairly and honestly. If you want to reap the rewards of the market, you have to treat your customers and suppliers just the same.

Social pressure – the threat of losing your reputation, for example – is usually enough to ensure that people follow the rules. But not always: if people don't pay their bills, repair faults or meet their contracts, then some stronger enforcement is needed. Then, we resort to the power of the state, with its police, its courts and its punishments.

> *National markets are held together by shared values and confidence in certain minimum standards. But in the new global market, people do not yet have that confidence.*
>
> **– Former UN Secretary-General Kofi Annan, 1999**

The state is the ultimate *enforcer* of the rules of market behaviour. But it *makes* some of these rules too. It writes the standards of behaviour into law, crystallizing the existing, unwritten rules. And sometimes it creates new rules.

Usually the aim is to make the market work more efficiently – with anti-monopoly regulation, say, or standardized weights and measures. Many legislatures insist that goods sold should be safe and fit for purpose, which helps lift the *caveat emptor* burden of constant vigilance from consumers, and strengthens the bond of trust between buyers and sellers. Regulatory control of complicated services – such as banking, insurance or pensions – may likewise increase customers' confidence and so allow these markets to expand.

Sometimes the aim may be to ban or regulate some trade that is considered damaging or immoral – narcotics or gambling, for instance, or selling yourself into slavery (a rule invoked by many a rising rock group trying to escape from onerous recording contracts).

THE UNWRITTEN RULES

So the state has become a maker of rules, as well as their enforcer. Yet most market transactions remain based on trust and human understanding, rather than on contracts and legal rules. That is how I am able to get my hems fixed by someone I don't know and whose language I cannot speak. It's how I can take a taxi ride or order a pizza without signing a contract to assure the driver or the chef that I will pay. Even though we're strangers, we don't need to discuss payment or sign contracts – we all just *know* what is expected from each side.

We do it the easy way because it works.

It's much easier to work on the basis of trust, which is why doing so has become a part of our culture. Of course, there can be problems when cultures clash: American smokers used to be staggered when asked to pay for matches in British pubs. And I never quite knew whether I was being charged for the water, bread rolls and other extras that I was offered in American restaurants. But in general we do it this way, the easy way, because it *works*.

As social creatures, cooperation comes naturally to us. The dog eat dog idea of the market is wide of the mark. It's not human: it's not even rational. Markets are not a series of one-off transactions with complete strangers, whom you can cheat with impunity. The best way to make money is to run a business that your customers trust, and keep coming back to, so you have a steady, reliable stream of trade. You make yourself better off by consistently cooperating with others, not by trying to rob them.

PROPERTY INCLUDES HUMAN EFFORT

Markets are about the exchange of *property*. You exchange something you own, some piece of property, for something owned by another person, which you want more.

It isn't always physical property, like antiques, cars or televisions, that we exchange. Our *labour* is a form of property too. My main investment in the antique business was not the materials I used, but the time and skill that I spent on finding, cleaning, restoring, and selling my prints. I would not have gone to all that effort unless I thought that I would benefit by pocketing Mr Wildman's cheque at the end of it.

> **Human effort is the kind of property that we most commonly exchange.**

In fact this human effort is the kind of property we most commonly exchange. Most of us are employees: we sell our time and skill for cash. Even if we do live by selling property – antiques, say – it is generally our time and skill that are the most valuable elements of it. Mr Wildman sold antiques; but much of their price was actually compensation for his time, judgement, knowledge and years of experience in the trade.

This is why the law protects people's *intellectual* property as well as their physical property. The effort and ingenuity, or sheer good luck, to compose a hit melody or develop a new industrial process are safeguarded from theft through copyright and patents, just as surely as your home or your lottery winnings are.

PROPERTY SECURITY IS VITAL TO MARKETS

If you are going into an exchange, you want to be sure not only that you are getting the *right* property – a genuine antique, for example – but that you will get to enjoy it too. If you think your property is simply going to be stolen from you, there is not much point in making the effort to trade.

This explains why so many poor countries remain poor. Why should people bother to build up capital such as farms, buildings or equipment, if those things are likely to be nationalized, raided by hostile armies, or stolen from them by gangsters or corrupt politicians? And if they do decide not to bother, the whole country suffers as jobs and production are lost.

This is why so many poor countries remain poor.

Things are little better when property is commonly owned. China's collective farms had miserable productivity because nobody saw any point in working hard when any benefit that resulted would be shared with everyone else, hard working or lazy. The sensible plan was to take it easy and let others exert themselves. Only when the rules changed and families took charge of their own plots did things improve – rapidly and dramatically.

It is the *tragedy of the commons*: nobody feels inclined to look after something when they get only a small part of the benefit in return. It's why collective farms don't work, why fishing grounds are always over-fished, and why the common stairways in apartment blocks are so badly decorated and maintained.

PROPERTY RIGHTS ARE DETERMINED BY LAW AND CONVENTION

So if markets are to work, what *property rights* should you enjoy?

First, you must be able to *hold* property: when you buy a house, a set of written deeds confirms your ownership. Second, you must be able to *exclude others* from it: when you own the house, you can legitimately prevent people from wandering into the garden and picking the flowers. Third, you must be able to *enjoy what your property produces*: any income you can get from renting out your house, for example, or the fruit from your apple trees. And fourth, you must be able to *alienate* your property again: in other words, you can *sell* your house and pass all these rights on to someone else.

> *Social convention may limit how we use our property.*

But laws and social conventions set limits on these rights. Owning a house does not allow you to prevent aircraft flying over it; regulation might restrict what you can charge in rent; in some countries the law prevents you from selling your house to foreigners; and even if it's legal to store rubbish on your front lawn, your neighbours' reaction might convince you not to.

Of course, there may be sensible reasons for such restraints: air travel would be impossible if airlines had to get everyone's permission to fly over their gardens. But in general, the weaker that property rights are made, the less well do markets function – as when property owners refuse to rent out apartments because regulation puts a limit on what they can charge.

THE CHOICE OF RULES DETERMINES THE OUTCOME

Precisely what happens in a market, then, depends on how these rules of property and exchange are framed. When the ruler's friends are given a monopoly on salt, we can all expect to pay more for salt. Regulated taxis (like London's, where drivers have to use the standard 'black cab' and possess the comprehensive 'knowledge' of the streets) will be higher quality but more expensive and less plentiful than unregulated ones. And when the rules change rapidly – when governments suddenly deregulate the aviation or telecoms sector, for example – markets can go into turmoil before they eventually settle down in some new order.

Another rule that changes the market – hopefully for the better – is *limited liability*. This is where the owners of a business are liable only for what they have invested in it. That puts suppliers at a small risk: if the company goes bust they might not get paid. But it spares entrepreneurs the much bigger risk of having to sell their homes and possessions to repay creditors. As such, it encourages people to take entrepreneurial risks from which we all benefit, without fearing that a mistake could ruin them forever.

THE DESIGN OF AUCTIONS

Different kinds of *auction* show how different rules affect market outcomes differently. Auctions are useful when we are not quite sure what something is worth to buyers: not for everyday items like bread or cheese, where prices are well established, but for rare paintings, used cars and farmland, where buyers' interest can be more variable.

In the familiar English auction system of open bidding, the price is bid up until only one bidder is left. That provides useful information to buyers, enabling them to see what other people think the object is worth. In a Dutch auction, by contrast, the price is successively lowered until one bidder accepts it. But that gives buyers no opportunity to know if others are interested – until it's too late.

Then there are sealed bid auctions, where people submit bids that are unknown to other bidders until the auction closes and they are all opened. But bidding in the dark like this can unsettle buyers, who have no way of knowing whether other people are interested, and so whether they are massively under- or overbidding.

Precisely for that reason, some auctions are second-price auctions. Again, the bids are sealed, but the winner

The ingenious 3G auction

In 2000, nobody knew what 3G mobile communications licences would be worth, because the technology was novel. In a sealed-bid auction, people might have bid cautiously, having no idea what anyone else thought each licence might be worth. Instead, the sale structure was ingeniously designed and netted the UK government around £30 billion, ten times the amount originally anticipated.

There were five licences, one more than the number of mobile telecoms operators, so new providers came into the market, increasing the competition for the rights. Five licences would not give anyone a monopoly, but would restrict competition enough for bidders to know that they could make reasonable returns, increasing the licences' value once again.

The auction worked through round after round of bidding (almost a hundred of them): after each round, the participants could see what their rivals thought each licence was worth, and guess their plans, giving each of them the confidence to raise their bids on the next round.

pays only the amount bid by the second-highest bidder. This gives everyone more confidence that they won't end up paying a price that is dramatically out of line with what others think the object is worth – the so-called 'winner's curse'.

By cleverly designing the rules of an auction, sellers can give buyers the confidence – and make them sense enough competition – to get a better price for what they are selling. The rules of the market *matter*.

MARKETS DON'T JUST HAPPEN

Markets, then, exist only within a framework of rules – legal rules and social norms too – which establish the exact nature of property rights and govern how property is exchanged. Exactly how these rules are framed can make a big difference to the outcome: but it is not always easy to find the best set of rules, because the issues can be difficult.

Are my property rights being violated, for example, if the smell from your factory drifts onto my neighbouring farm? Or my restaurant? Should anglers have the right to prevent passing motorboats disturbing the fish, or should boaters have priority? But these are issues for the next chapter.

CHAPTER SEVEN

Market Failure (and Government Failure)

BUBBLES, BOOMS, DOWNTURNS AND DEPRESSIONS

Folk who had small children back in 1982 still shudder. That was the year of America's great Cabbage Patch Kids hysteria. The cloth dolls became the must-have Christmas gift for youngsters. Every kid wanted one. Parents lined up at toy stores. Large numbers were sold. The lines got longer, and the shelves emptier. Some stores ran out, and customers trawled store after store to find them. Rumours about fresh deliveries spread like wildfire. Parents would converge on the lucky store, standing for hours in the winter snow if need be. As supplies neared exhaustion, there was panic, even violence. By the time Christmas came around, large numbers of potential customers remained disappointed, not to mention tired and bruised.

Five years later, the speculator George Soros wrote a book saying that the financial markets were just as crazy. Everybody, he said, rushes to buy a popular stock and to ditch one they fear might fall, which just exaggerates the rise or fall even more. Markets, he concluded, seem to be in a permanent state of imbalance, producing bubbles, booms, downturns and depressions.

MARKETS STRUGGLE WITH HUMAN PSYCHOLOGY

Many people think we can't have faith in markets, precisely because they produce such wild swings as these. But then markets are only human; they rest on human psychology—how human beings deal with their different values.

And human interaction of any sort can often produce some odd results. If people think things will become scarce, everybody rushes to buy them, just in case they run out – which, of course, they then do. When the media warn that this year's must-have toy will be hard to get, or experts predict that a particular stock will skyrocket, the fear of losing out produces a stampede in which many people do indeed miss out.

> *Markets are only human, and about human psychology.*

People call things like this *market failure*. But actually it's a *human* failing, or just a human trait. We are social creatures. We like to be in with the crowd. We follow the fashion. We want to be part of the latest craze. So when we are told that something is selling well, we all want to buy it too, and suppliers are overwhelmed.

Of course, suppliers could respond by raising their prices. That would curb demand, and encourage new suppliers to come in to capture the new high prices for themselves. But that's not always possible. A toy store that raised the price of its Cabbage Patch Kids by ten or twenty times might succeed in being able to supply every customer who was prepared to pay that much – though it would undoubtedly be accused of 'exploitation' by its regular customers, who might resolve never to shop there again. And in many countries, there are regulations that forbid shop owners from raising the price of goods once they have been advertised at a lower price, even if customers are rioting to get in.

TIME AND SPEED

A lot of the problem behind these sorts of 'failure' is merely that nobody can accurately forecast the future. If manufacturers knew, a year ahead, that Cabbage Patch Kids would be in huge demand, they could simply make more. But there is no way of predicting this. Entrepreneurs just have to make a guess and take a risk. And different entrepreneurs will guess differently.

> *A market is the combined behaviour of thousands of people responding to information, misinformation and whim.*
> – *New York Times* **science writer Kenneth Chang**

Take the dotcom boom of the 1990s. The new information technology was reckoned to be as important as the invention of electricity – it would completely revolutionize commerce. The potential investment rewards could be huge. So vast numbers of people joined the herd and decided it was worth a punt. The bubble grew. But in fact the rewards turned out to be lower than the more optimistic forecasts, and were concentrated in a small number of enterprising and well-managed companies which used the new technology to advantage. The boom subsided. Can you really blame 'the market', though, if people act on what they think will happen – but it doesn't?

Information about what actually *is* happening doesn't travel at internet speeds, either. It takes time to get round a market. It has to be discovered, extracted, thought about, processed and acted on. That doesn't happen in an instant. When, after a period of rising prices, the leading market insiders have sensed things are turning and sold their stock, other people still pile in to it because the information that things are cooling hasn't got to them yet, or because the information they do have is simply wrong.

> *Stock market bubbles don't grow out of thin air. They have a solid basis in reality, but reality as distorted by a misconception.*
> **– Investment guru George Soros**

Of this are bubbles made. They usually have a basis in reality: the reality that something is getting scarce. But this state of affairs is sometimes exaggerated, not just by human beings' desire to be part of the crowd, but by the fact that the people are basing their actions on faulty information.

Can you really blame the market system for that? It's like a motorway pile-up. If everyone saw that the car twelve vehicles ahead had stopped, they'd all apply the brakes gently now. But all they see is the car in front stopping abruptly and themselves going into the back of it. You can't blame the car or the road. You should blame the drivers.

INFORMATION ASYMMETRY

Another thing that makes it hard for markets to work properly is what economists call *information asymmetry*. That's when one person in an exchange has a lot more information than the other. It's why you can't buy a decent second-hand car, except maybe from dealers. Dealers would lose reputation if they sold you a dud car; but you don't have that safety net when you buy from a private owner, who has no reputation at stake. Worse, when private owners find a good car, they hang on to it: they only sell the duds. As a buyer, you can't know, from a brief inspection, that you're getting a dud; so you agree to buy it, and the seller smirks inwardly. That's information asymmetry.

Or take health insurance. People don't often buy health insurance when they feel healthy: they buy it when they think they might develop some expensive medical condition. The trouble for insurers is that you (and millions like you) know more about your own state of health than they ever could, sitting in an office miles away. If they took everyone who applied, they would find themselves insuring a lot of expensive, unhealthy people and few healthy ones. So to level up the information playing field, they might give you a medical check-up. Your information edge costs them money.

Information asymmetry can be a real pest.

Even if they take you on, their problems are not over. If you fall ill, your doctor may suggest all sorts of expensive tests. The insurers, who will have to pay for them, may not be happy: but the doctor has more information than they do about what is appropriate in your particular case. The insurers could demand a second opinion, but that would cost them still more money.

Insurers have other ways round the information asymmetry problem, such as forcing you to pay a portion of any medical costs, so that you don't willingly volunteer for pointless tests. But it's a cat-and-mouse game. The result is that insured people get medical treatment they don't really need, or the cost of insurance goes up and up, or both.

But that's information asymmetry for you: resources tend to end up with the person who's better informed, rather than the one who values those resources more strongly. Information asymmetry can be a real pest.

POLITICAL FAILURE

The thing that really messes up the efficient allocation of resources to their most valued uses is not market failure, though. It's *political failure*.

Markets are a lot more nimble than the political process. We get to vote only every few years. Even then, it's on a whole package of measures – the cost of living, defence, employment, crime and much else. But the market is a sort of daily election, on specific products. When you buy a particular bar of chocolate, you send manufacturers an instant message on what kind of chocolate you prefer, and where and when you want it, and at what price. You send the same, daily, instant messages with everything you buy.

Governments, then, can't outperform markets; but when markets produce results that voters don't like, politicians are nevertheless called on to intervene. Whatever it is – low wages, high prices – people demand that governments should 'do something'. Just as markets struggle with asymmetric information, though, the political system fails because of asymmetric interests. Small groups with a lot to gain from government intervention are its loudest advocates; large groups with only a little to lose do not register much of a protest.

Suppose that farmers are having a difficult time. They may demand government subsidies on the grounds that food is essential and that if farmers go bust it leaves us at the mercy of foreign imports. It's worth them campaigning stridently, because there are few of them and a subsidy would make them much better off. Of course, the subsidy requires taxpayers to pay for it. But since there are a lot of taxpayers, the burden is widely spread. It's not really worth any of the general public getting worked up about something that has a very small effect on their tax bill.

The trouble happens when there are lots of small groups, all campaigning for preferential treatment. The cost on

> ## Why government just grows
> When I worked for the US Congress, I was astonished that the Food Stamp Bill (a welfare measure) was tacked on the end of the Farm Bill. Then I realized: the Democrats disliked farm subsidies, but desperately wanted more welfare for their inner-city voters. The Republicans disliked welfare but desperately wanted farm subsidies for their rural voters. Put subsidies and welfare together, and they both vote for the package.
>
> What's called *public choice theory* explains the detail of such things, but in reality it's easy: you vote for my measure, I'll vote for yours. The politicians all get what they want. Unfortunately, in the process, voters get more government than they *ever* wanted.

taxpayers rises, but in tiny, almost unnoticeable increments. Before long, though, a large amount of money has left the pockets of the general public and gone into those of vested interest groups. In modern politics, such extortion has become quite an art.

THE INCONVENIENT REALITY
On Mondays, if the house shook, my job was to run out and bring in the washing. Pulling off the wooden dolly pegs, I would put the wet clothes into my mother's wicker

washing basket (easily big enough for both me and a primary-school friend to sit in) and drag it indoors. The jolt, and the bang that went with it, meant that the local quarry was blasting, and that a cloud of dust could be heading in our direction, depositing a thin layer of dust on our wet clothes. In fact, it was only a problem on washing days when the breeze blew from the Northeast, which it rarely did. People fifty miles away in the industrial 'Black County' (the name given to the coal-rich Midlands of England) had a much worse problem, with the constant smuts and smoke from nearby factory chimneys.

Many people can't see how markets can deal with so-called *externalities* like pollution, not to mention traffic congestion, water shortages, over-fishing, wildlife protection and other environmental problems. So they demand that governments step in – with emissions standards for cars and factories, new roads and public infrastructure, or bans on fishing and hunting.

Unfortunately, such obvious measures can create more problems than they solve.

Regulation is a sledgehammer that misses the nut.

If factories belch out smoke that drifts into neighbours' gardens, why *not* just tell them they can no longer do it? The answer is that it doesn't necessarily make sense, because there's a downside too. Perhaps some factories could install clean-up technology; but they would have to charge customers more for what they produce. Others might have processes that simply can't be cleaned up: they would have to close, and their product (and local jobs) would be lost. Regulation is a sledgehammer that misses the nut.

How do we know whether people value the fall in pollution more than the increased price of the products or the loss of local jobs? We don't. That's the sort of problem you need a *market* to solve. But too often, instead of trying to develop a market in which different people's values could be measured and balanced, we resort to regulation, and actually prevent any market from being established.

A regulation that simply prohibited factories from emitting smoke would be costly and would probably not deliver what people actually wanted. But what if we established a market, requiring factory owners to pay their neighbours in proportion to the amount of smoke they produced? Pretty soon the two sides would agree a price for the nuisance caused. Harmony would break out: the factories could continue producing at least some smoke, and neighbours would regard themselves as adequately compensated for it. And the fact that the factories were paying for any smoke they produced would give them a good incentive to invest in clean-up technology or to look for cleaner production processes – which is what we want.

In other words, the problem is not so much that markets have *failed*, as that they don't *exist*. And we would be better to try to create them, rather than just banning things and preventing markets from ever existing.

A MARKET IN EMISSIONS

Actually, many people now see the merit of getting the power of the market onside, and have developed ideas such as *tradable emissions permits*. In this system, the community decides how much pollution it will tolerate over the local area. It then issues permits totalling this amount, and divides them between local businesses. Businesses that cannot cut their emissions then have to buy permits from those who can. If you can cut your emissions, you can sell your permits and pocket the money. It's a very positive market incentive to get clean.

The United States launched this system in 1995, allowing companies to trade permits in sulphur dioxide emissions (produced mainly by coal-fired power generators). The results exceeded expectation, and brokerage firms sprang up, making it easy for firms to trade permits. Europe now has its own carbon-trading scheme: it's too politicized but still an improvement over the traditional all-or-nothing regulation.

A PRICE ON CONGESTION

Traffic congestion is another problem caused by the absence of a market. Once you have bought and taxed your vehicle, there's nothing to discourage you from driving down the busiest road in the busiest district at the busiest time. But in doing so, you add to the congestion and cause problems for everyone else – wasted time, missed appointments and more accidents.

Again, the answer is to use market principles – to put a price on using busy roads at peak times. Singapore did that in 1975, requiring motorists to pay a daily charge for entering the business area of the city. It cut congestion and allowed traffic to move faster. Norway, too, introduced road pricing in three cities, using the revenues to improve roads, pedestrian bridges and cycle lanes. Central London's charge, introduced in 2003, also eased congestion.

These systems are all crude. They involve drawing a boundary round an area and charging people to cross it. That makes the system easy to understand, though it can't smooth out the traffic as well as one that charges people for travelling on individual streets according to how busy they are – which would incentivize drivers to find the least congested routes and times.

WATER RIGHTS

Water may be essential to life, but in many places it is also very scarce. We want everyone to have access to it, but we don't want it wasted.

Unfortunately, public policy often kills off market solutions here too. In the western United States, for example, the 'prior appropriation' rule meant that those who first started to extract water from a stream long ago got priority over those coming later. That prompted people to extract water they didn't need, just to keep this right active. Other rules that water should go to 'beneficial use' meant that water for fish, wildlife and other public purposes became particularly scarce.

So why not treat water like any other resource and create a market in it? In the early 1990s, this idea took hold, and states began allowing people to trade their water rights. Montana allowed people to lease water rights to maintain stream flows for fish. Arizona looked at how to market its unused share of Colorado River water to California and Nevada. The water rights market now stretches throughout the West, from Washington to Texas and from California to Colorado. Again, it's not perfect and there are legal challenges, but it's making water allocation more efficient.

Water metering can do the same job for domestic water supplies. If water is paid for through taxation, there is no incentive to fix a leaky tap or stop watering the lawn, since you pay the same no matter how much you use. If your supply is metered, though, there is every incentive. When large-scale metering was introduced in the United Kingdom in 1988, consumption in the affected areas fell about 10%. And social concerns can be built into the price – with a certain free allowance for everyone, for example, and people paying only for what they use above that.

The free rider problem

For many years, economists considered lighthouses an almost perfect example of a 'public good' – something useful which the market just couldn't supply. After all, if ships 'free ride' and leave others to pay, they get the same benefit at no cost.

In fact, ship owners have always understood the need to pay for lighthouses. In 1722 the owners of ships passing by the Channel Islands asked the owner of dangerous rocks nearby to build the Casquets Lighthouse – for which they would pay a fee, according to their tonnage. Other lighthouses were also privately financed, through fees charged to ships tying up at nearby harbours – a practice which goes back to 1261.

Even where it is impossible to exclude free riders, private philanthropy can help pay for a service. Britain's Royal National Lifeboat Institution, created in 1824, remains a huge success, even though it takes no government money. From 1854, it did take government funds, but found that it lost more in private donations than it gained from state subsidies. So in 1869 it cut loose. It's now the UK's twelfth-largest charity, maintaining over 300 lifeboats and rescuing some 6000 people a year.

TRADABLE FISHING RIGHTS

Over-fishing is one of those *tragedy of the commons* problems, where nobody really owns the resource, so everyone uses it free of charge, until it is exhausted. The market has again found solutions.

Scotland is world famous for its salmon streams. It's not because Scottish salmon are better than anywhere else (whatever the Scots say). It is because the rights to fish every inch of every river in Scotland are privately owned. The owners make a good business of issuing fishing permits to anglers, and so have a strong incentive to keep the rivers clean and well stocked.

Just as any landowner can exclude trespassers, so the owners of fishing rights in Scotland can legally exclude others from their particular stretch of water. These valuable rights are jealously guarded: poaching is not considered quite as bad as high treason, but it's close. And considerable funds are spent in maintaining this market. When a hydro-electric dam was built at the Highland town of Pitlochry, for example, an elaborate 'salmon ladder' was constructed alongside – a gentle cascade of water tanks that allow the salmon to swim upstream and over the dam. Their jumping from tank to tank is now a tourist attraction in its own right.

The result is that Scotland's salmon rivers are well maintained and not over-fished. Indeed, a few years ago a private trust purchased a number of downstream fishing rights and retired them – issuing no fishing permits – specifically in order to increase salmon stocks for the upstream sport fishing industry. The market nurtures the environment.

OVER-FISHING

Markets can even work in sea fishing. Faced with declining stocks of cod and other species in the North Sea, the European Union tried several solutions. First, it ruled that fishing boats had to remain tied up for a number of days a year. But that just meant that valuable capital was sitting in port, doing nothing. And on the days the boats were allowed to go out, they tried to make up for lost time by catching even more fish. A second solution was to set quotas on the amount of cod that fishing boats could land. But boats looking for other species unintentionally netted cod too, and had to throw the over-quota dead cod back into the sea – a sad waste of resources.

Iceland has had a lot more success, using market principles. In 1983, it set a limit on the total volume of fish that could be caught around Iceland, and issued tradable quotas to the fishing boats – rather like the pollution permit idea. The individual quotas are valuable property. The more efficient boats buy them from the less efficient ones, making the whole industry more cost-effective. You can even sell part of your quota: so if you want to fish less this year but more next year, you can sell part of your quota now and buy part of someone else's next year. It's a market-based model that conserves resources – and now other countries are looking at similar systems.

A SHOOTING MARKET SAVES GAME

Poaching might be akin to treason in Scotland, but it is routine in some parts of Africa: rhino are poached for their precious horn, and villagers don't flinch from shooting elephants, which they see as a costly crop-destroying nuisance. So how can we protect these rare species?

The obvious policy – punishing anyone caught killing them – does not work. Villagers will risk it, rather than see their harvest trampled underfoot, and policing such large areas is impossible. But the market has a solution: make the very rarity of these animals the basis for a business. Now, in game lodges across southern Africa, visitors come and pay to hunt (or just to watch and photograph), rhino, elephant, lion and many other species. Quotas for shooting are set in relation to the species' reproduction and maturity rates, and usually the lodges will steer shooters to the older animals. The visitors pay handsomely to take home an elephant trophy, and the money goes back into protecting and conserving the existing stocks.

Now the local villagers see elephants as a source of income, not a pest: they dig water holes for them in times of drought, and use electric fences, rather than bullets, to protect their crops. In several countries, this market-driven policy has led to a revival in many species that were once seriously threatened.

Even here, then, where you would not expect market principles to apply, they turn out to be both relevant and effective. In addition, the outcome is one that most people would say is morally better. But then the market system is a surprisingly *moral* system.

CHAPTER EIGHT

The Morality of the Market

The first time I went to the Baltic state of Estonia, it was hard to get something for lunch. The place was still under Russian control, and the old Soviet ways persisted.

My host knew several restaurants in Tallinn, so we set off. At the first, the door was locked shut, but he knocked on it loudly. Nothing happened. So he knocked again, longer this time. After the third bout of knocking, a sleepy-eyed waiter opened the door and explained that they had no food.

The explanation sounded quite plausible. The only thing we ever got to eat in Estonia was a sort of stew made from spicy sausages, followed by jell-o. Decent food was obviously in short supply. But my friend explained the real problem: they didn't want to serve us.

At the next restaurant – I would not have realized it was a restaurant, because it had no signs to attract customers – another locked door confronted us. There was more vigorous knocking before it was opened. I can't remember what the excuse was this time, but again, we didn't get in.

Customers were merely an inconvenience to be avoided.

At the third place, my friend knocked firmly, and rapped hard on the window too. This time we were told that the restaurant was full. I don't know how my host, speaking

Estonian, countered this; but after a minute or so of argument on the doorstep, we were actually admitted. We sat down, and the waiter handed us menus, before explaining that all they had was sausage stew and jell-o.

The place wasn't full. In fact, we were the only people there. What my friend had said of the first place was true of them all: they simply didn't want to serve us. And why should they? Under the system then in place, they got paid whether they had any customers or not. They would much prefer to sit around, smoking and playing cards, than to serve customers. Customers were merely an inconvenience to be avoided.

HARNESSING SELF-INTEREST

Today there are countless restaurants in Tallinn, all of which have open doors and welcome you in. The credit for Estonia's recovery belongs to Mart Laar, the young prime minister who turned Estonia into a market economy. In the Soviet period, he explains, the only Western economics book he was able to lay his hands on was *Free to Choose* by Milton and Rose Friedman – which extols the virtues of free markets. Not having read the mainstream Western textbooks, he had never been told that these ideas were impracticable. So he went ahead and did them, and they succeeded.

And which scenario is more moral: the old one where people consciously avoided giving service to others, or the new one where they positively welcome the chance? I have no doubt. It's the new one.

The old system, certainly, was built on moral ideas like equality, public service and selflessness. But it did nothing to counter the natural human trait of laziness, nor harness that of self-interest, as the market system does. It assumed that people's enthusiastic pursuit of a socialist society would eclipse such vices. As I discovered in Estonia, it didn't.

SELF-INTEREST AND GREED

Nevertheless, many people still think the market system can never be moral because it is rooted in self-interest, and self-interest is a vice.

This confuses *self-interest*, which is a perfectly natural, and indeed necessary human characteristic, with *greed*, which is undoubtedly a vice. In fact, a certain level of self-interest is essential to life: if none of us looked after ourselves, our society would be in a very sorry state. We eat, drink and clothe ourselves because that's what we need to survive and to be contented. It's self-interest, right enough, but it's hardly a vice. We can look after our own interests and still be honest, reliable, just and pleasant. These things are not incompatible.

I suppose you could say that my father started his village car-repair business for reasons of self-interest. It was a way of earning money that he could spend on the things he really wanted. He also liked fixing cars. But equally, he thought it was a *useful* and *worthwhile* thing to do. I don't think he had an atom of greed in his body, any more than did the village shopkeeper two doors away, the couple who ran the public house opposite or the butcher up at the crossroads. In fact, if anyone in the village had thought them greedy, they would all have lost people's trust and had fewer customers as a result.

> *You have to serve other people's interests in order to serve your own.*

In markets, if you want to serve your own self-interest, you can do it only by delivering some benefit to others in exchange. You have to serve other people's interests in order to serve your own. But you can't do that by greedily trying to exploit others: maybe you could pocket a quick profit by selling shoddy goods, but word would spread and soon you would have no business left. You would be better to deliver excellent value so that customers keep coming back and recommending you to friends.

By encouraging each of us to serve others in this way, the market makes us promote the interests of the community as a whole. Far from being a vice, the market system makes self-interest into something thoroughly virtuous.

HARMONY VERSUS POLITICS

Indeed, the market facilitates peaceful cooperation on an international scale. As with Adam Smith's example of the woollen coat, even the simplest product may contain the work of people from many countries. Market exchange enables millions of people to cooperate, even those who come from different lands, speak different languages and have different – even conflicting – ideas, values and opinions. I buy Iranian dates because they are delicious: in doing so I put money into the purses of Iranian date farmers, though I have little in common with them and don't like their government one bit.

Markets are our most powerful tool to promote cooperation between disparate and possibly hostile people. Indeed, the more divergently people value things, the more benefit they each derive from exchange, and the more likely they are to trade. The more they do, the more stake they have in preserving the peace that makes possible that trade and its benefits.

> **When goods do not cross borders, soldiers will.**
> **– Nineteenth-century French economist and politician Frédéric Bastiat**

Some critics imagine that a system built on the tension between buyers and sellers – and the competition between buyers and between sellers – must inevitably involve more conflict than one where resources are allocated by majority agreement. But when things are decided through the political process, the potential for conflict is *greater*, because the stakes are higher. The political decision to adopt one plan for national production means that all others must be abandoned. For the potential losers, the decision is worth fighting, particularly since it may not be revisited until the next election. That's why public-sector services are so frequently dogged by strikes and disruptions.

> ***Markets are our most powerful tool to promote cooperation.***

The market, by contrast, produces a wide variety of goods and services that simultaneously serve even conflicting tastes. And such conflicts that arise are continuously and automatically resolved. Greater competition for the same resource raises its price, whereupon some buyers will buy less and use it more sparingly, or drop out of the market entirely and switch to cheaper alternatives. It's a daily process of gradual adjustment to the realities of supply and demand, and it happens for every single good and service. That's much less divisive than when a whole raft of production decisions is made only as the result of infrequent elections or votes in the legislature.

UNFAIRNESS AND INEQUALITY

The market may reduce conflict, but does it produce fair results? Critics argue that nurses who tend the sick are paid maybe a hundredth as much as top entertainers who tend only their own bank accounts. How can that be just?

But wages – like any other prices – are simply the outcome of an impersonal system of rules. Like the outcome of a game of chess, they are neither just nor unjust – they are simply a fact. There are very few talented entertainers, and millions of people are prepared to pay them handsomely for what they do. There are many people who could become nurses, but they can care for only a few patients at a time, so are much less well paid. Yet nobody has acted unfairly or unjustly. The result is merely what voluntary exchange produces.

> *The inherent vice of capitalism is the unequal sharing of the blessings. The inherent blessing of socialism is the equal sharing of misery.*
>
> **– Former UK Prime Minister Winston Churchill**

Even with such obvious differences, market societies are actually more equal than others. Inequalities are greatest where it's power, not money, which counts. Anyone can pursue wealth: but power elites are open to just a few who have the right family, race, attitudes or religion.

And there is more social mobility in market economies: people may be rich or poor, but they aren't doomed to remain so. Young people might work for low wages in fast-food places, but as they gain experience and qualifications, they can move on to more interesting, better-paid work. My student business of selling antique prints didn't exactly net me a fortune; but it taught me a lot about work and business that made it possible for me to earn more later on. You have to look at the dynamics of an economy, not just at a snapshot; and market economies are highly dynamic.

Governments may try to reduce inequalities by taxing wealthier people and subsidizing poorer ones. But there's a cost: by reducing people's rewards, you reduce their motivation to steer their effort to where it is needed. And there's a moral cost too: people have to be *coerced* into paying taxes.

TRAFFICKING AND EXPLOITATION

Some say that the lure of profit encourages crimes such as trafficking in drugs, weapons and even human beings. But you cannot blame the market for such crimes, any more than you can blame politics for the crime of ballot rigging. People, not organizational systems, commit crimes. If anything, it is not the lure of profit in a *free* society that makes people criminals, rather their efforts to escape the oppression of a *coercive* one.

And what about exploitation? Critics argue, for example, that the market economy forces people in developing countries to work long hours making cheap shoes or clothes, at a fraction of the wages that would be acceptable in wealthier countries.

But then people are not *forced* to work in these conditions. They do so because the alternative is very much worse – maybe twelve hours a day of hard manual work under the hot sun in waterlogged, mosquito-infested rice fields.

The pay in a Nike shoe factory in Vietnam may be low by Western standards, but it's regular, and many times the uncertain and meagre living from subsistence agriculture. After two or three years of it, workers can afford bicycles to spare themselves the walk to work; after a bit more, maybe a scooter. Before long, they start extending and improving their homes, arranging proper education for their children, and even creating their own small businesses that will keep them and their community out of poverty for all time. It's for reasons like these that Vietnam's communist government has actually hailed Nike as an example of a good and responsible business.

THE DOMINATION OF BIG BUSINESS

Karl Marx, the intellectual pioneer of communism, did not expect it all to work out like this. He thought that what economists call *economies of scale* – the fact that you can mass-produce thousands of widgets much more cheaply than you can hand-make just a few – would force businesses to grow larger and larger in order to see off the competition. Eventually they would see off *all* the competition, and we would be left with just a few monopolies, which could then exploit the workers.

But, 150 years on, it hasn't happened.

The nearest thing to a celebrity in my family was my grandfather, who appeared – unnamed – on the cover of a 1948 issue of *Picture Post*, illustrating an article about training gundogs, his profession. A flick through the advertisements in this magazine shows just how wrong Marx was. There are firms selling cider, radios, rat poison, bile beans, a 'shampoo to the stars', floor polishers, sauces, soap, cycles, surgical dressings, dog food, shaving cream and peas. They were the big firms of 1948, but none of them even exist today, any more than *Picture Post* itself does. It hasn't been a remorseless progress towards monopoly, just constant change: big firms being challenged by new competitors with better products, who are in turn challenged by others. That doesn't *exploit* the public – it *benefits* them.

> *Underlying most arguments against the free market is a lack of belief in freedom itself.*
>
> **– Nobel economist Milton Friedman**

Certainly, there are big multinationals in some sectors where scale is an advantage – oil, mining, car making, pharmaceuticals, media and so on. These sectors demand big investments, so it is no surprise that large players dominate them. In a decade or two it will be a different set, though – just as Japanese, Korean and now Chinese manufacturers have eclipsed the once-dominant car industries of Britain or America.

And there is still competition from a lot of niche players as well – specialist film producers, custom carmakers. For a time, I myself was in the oil business – one of a group of academics in Hillsdale College, Michigan, who chipped in to invest in the local 'wildcat' oil prospectors. 'Big oil' might be big, but it's not exactly a monopoly.

LIMITS TO MARKET DOMINATION

In any case, markets are not about selling identical products where economies of scale apply. They are about trying to get an edge over other sellers by differentiating your product from theirs. Rather than churning out vast quantities of identical products, the struggle to be different means continual innovation and change and renewal. The bigger your investment in some production process, the harder you fall when some smart newcomer makes it redundant.

There are also *dis*economies of scale. For instance, it's a lot easier to run a small company, where you can know all the staff personally and walk round the factory in a morning. In large firms, just communicating with a vast workforce or keeping track of the assets can be a hugely complex – and costly – business in itself.

It's also worth remembering that *services* are a growing share of modern economies. Services by their nature are more face-to-face and personal (think of dog groomers or house painters), and do not take readily to large-scale multinational provision.

Certainly, if the costs of doing business are high, market entry is difficult and only a few players exist, they might try to form a cartel to raise prices. That is precisely why we have laws to prevent them. But cartels are actually hard to maintain. It's too easy for members to cheat and cream off extra customers by offering a lower price than the agreed one – secretly if need be. Perhaps that's why the only people who've ever made an oil cartel stick for any length of time are not the commercial oil companies but the governments of oil-producing countries (ninety percent of which are not even democracies). The market can hardly be blamed for that.

THE MORAL SUPERIORITY OF MARKETS

Markets have their share of problems, but all in all, they seem to be to be far superior to the alternative – not just in terms of efficiency but in moral terms too. Non-market economies are steered by big, infrequent decisions made by political elites. Market economies are actually much more democratic, being driven by millions of small decisions made by each of us every single day. The non-market economy risks everything on a single plan for the future. The market economy spreads and reduces risk by allowing all of us to make and reconcile our own plans.

It should be no surprise that democracy and human freedom have fared badly under socialism. The enormous power that is needed to control an entire economy is difficult for any democratic body to restrain. How can you even mount an opposition when the government controls the supply of the paper you need for pamphlets, or the venues you need for meetings? When the government runs the schools, whose message is going to be taught?

And in such a system, who is likely to rise to the top? It will be those who are most ruthless at using the power that a centralized economy hands them. It is their views and ideology that will dominate. In the market economy, by contrast, nobody can prevent free thought: indeed, the market rewards fresh ideas.

Morally, as well as economically, markets must be the world's future. We need to grow them and nurture them. But that itself requires a good deal of human care and effort.

CHAPTER NINE

How to Grow a Market

ECONOMIC ACHIEVEMENT GETS REAL

As I emerge from the Metro station, I'm already in a kind of market. Old women sell magazines from wire racks. Others line the wall, holding up a pathetic stock – a single cardigan or a couple of scarves – as they try to replace the pensions that economic upheaval has wrenched away from them.

The crowd surges past and I'm swept into a grand plaza, with an enormous triumphal archway of stone, topped by heroic-scale bronze statues of a tractor driver and a farm girl joyfully holding up sheaves of wheat. Walking through, I'm in a grand avenue of astonishing size. Before me stands the magnificent Friendship Fountain – not working today, but still inspiring, its bronze cornucopia reminding us of the peace and plenty we (supposedly) owe to socialism. Beyond is the mighty Russia House – grandest of the many pavilions that line the avenue, each built in the different styles of their regions, from Armenia to the Arctic, from the Baltic to the Baring Sea.

Peeling murals of Lenin gaze down on stalls selling goods of every description.

This is Moscow's All-Russia Exhibition Centre. The Soviets built it as their grand Exhibition of Economic Achievements. It is still always called by its Soviet-era initials – VDNKh.

And now? It's part recreation ground, part funfair – and part market. Walk into any of the great pavilions and you are dazzled by bizarre collections of goods for sale. Peeling murals of Lenin, surrounded by happy farm workers, gaze down on aluminium and glass stalls selling goods of every description – cosmetics, mobile phones, jewellery, fabrics, audio players, knitting wool, cameras, clocks, belts, jackets, shoes, binoculars, fur coats, china, books, sunglasses, toys, bikes, souvenirs . . . It seems to sum up the triumph of the market over socialism.

> *The market came with the dawn of civilization and it is not an invention of capitalism. If it leads to improving the well-being of the people there is no contradiction with socialism.*
>
> **– Former Soviet leader Mikhail Gorbachev**

THE TRIUMPH OF THE MARKET?

Not quite. As the kids rollerblade round the imposing statue of Lenin, they also have to dodge the people with sandwich-boards advising you which pavilion to visit in order to get the best cameras, clothing or cosmetics. Because without them, you wouldn't know where to go. In any established market, the camera sellers would congregate in one place, the clothiers in another and the perfumers in a third. The pattern would have emerged over the decades, as sellers realized the benefit of sparing customers the search costs of going from one place to another in order to find what they wanted and to compare quality and prices.

True, there is at least one pavilion devoted to a single theme – a cavernous barrel-vaulted hall, with a painted-out quote by Lenin on one wall and a giant poster of a sunflower obscuring some Soviet hero on the other. It's full of stalls selling plants, seeds, bulbs, tubers, mowers, pots, watering cans and all kinds of gardening needs. The grandest stalls are near the entrance, where the footfall is greatest: they get smaller and more basic as you go through, until, as in Lanzhou, you find people sitting on blankets on the floor, a few vegetables for sale beside them. But even this pavilion is also home to an incongruous section of television sellers.

The Russians still haven't quite **got** *the market yet.*

It all makes me think that the Russians haven't quite *got* the market yet. Perhaps that is no surprise: markets are human institutions, and like any human relationship, they take time to grow. Yet in 1992, with the Berlin Wall gone, Russia suddenly abandoned the old Soviet price controls. They called it shock therapy, and hoped that proper markets would soon spring up. But the shock was too much. The price of basic items – long obscured by the Soviet controls – shot up, causing great distress to pensioners and poorer people. Traditional trading relationships were torn apart. Russia now had a *price system*, but whatever *trust* there was between economic partners slipped away. And because *property rights* and the rule of law were not properly established, new relationships couldn't form, and markets couldn't develop.

The privatization of the big state industries had problems too. Privatization vouchers were distributed to the population, but few people had much understanding of what share ownership meant, and most considered the state companies to be worthless anyway. But the firms were privatized with their old *monopolies* intact – and the 'oligarchs' who bought up the privatization vouchers very cheaply acquired enormous market power and wealth.

HANDBAGGING THE STATE

Margaret Thatcher had more success privatizing Britain's state industries in the 1980s, largely because she introduced *competition* at the same time, and because people in Britain understood property rights and the other rules that make markets work.

Britain's problems were smaller than Russia's, but the state still controlled the 'commanding heights' of the economy. About a third of the population lived in state housing. Each morning, we would wake up to the state radio station, switch on the light (powered by state-produced electricity), maybe ignite the state-produced gas under a state-produced steel pan and cook a state-regulated egg in state-produced water. Then as you took the state-run bus or your state-produced car (running on state-produced fuel) to the state train station, you might get stuck behind a state delivery-company truck parked outside the state bank. How you might wish that you could just pick up your state telephone and book yourself on the state airline to jet off (from the state airport, of course) to somewhere sunny.

All these industries were privatized (apart from the BBC, which at least faces more competition these days). But to grow these new markets needed careful design. Many state industries were too big to sell to a single buyer: they had to be split into shares and sold more widely to the general public. But even in a largely market economy like Britain, few people knew what share ownership meant, and a massive education campaign was required in advance of the first privatizations.

All these industries were privatized, apart from the BBC.

There were also incentives for people to hold on to their shares, rather than selling out at the first whiff of profit, in order to create a real sense of ownership and develop proper markets. Although most of the state industries retained much of their monopolies, competition was introduced wherever possible, often provoking a big shake-up in the structure of the companies after privatization.

Britain was lucky in that people there generally understood how markets worked, and respected their rules. Most of the countries of Eastern Europe also made the transition to a market economy fairly well, because the old market ideas had not been completely forgotten during the years of Soviet domination. For Russia, which went straight from a peasant economy to a communist one, transition was much harder, because no *culture* of market behaviour really existed.

Markets, like friendships, don't happen just because you want them to. They take work, and the conditions have to be right for them. If you are going to grow a market, you need to make sure those essential conditions are in place.

RECIPE FOR A SUCCESSFUL MARKET

The first essential is of course *voluntary exchange* – people have to be free to make bargains with others. It's not a market if you're forced into it. And it's remarkable how often governments prevent free exchange – banning it on moral or public interest grounds (remember Prohibition?), limiting it (such as banning Sunday shop opening), or muscling into it for their own gain.

Exchange of course implies *specialization,* where people focus on producing certain things, and can then exchange their surplus. And the wider it is, the better the market works. Regulation (such as professional licensure) can restrict it; but it is also less extensive in poorer countries, where people haven't yet built up the *capital* to enable them to specialize, and in remote communities, where the population is sparse and people have to do more things for themselves. On the Scottish island where I have a home, nearly everyone seems to have several jobs. A sign over a workshop near us advertised 'P MacArthur – Glazier and Undertaker'. There simply wasn't enough trade to justify specialization in either job. In the mainland city of Glasgow, however, there are over a hundred specialist undertakers, and more than eighty glaziers.

The second essential is the *price system*. Prices have to be free enough to respond to emerging pockets of surplus and scarcity, and so provide the incentive for people to switch their effort from the one to the other. If governments try to control prices – perhaps because they fear that rising prices would be unpopular among voters – markets can't grow properly. And as Russia found, it can be difficult to adjust once the controls are lifted.

The third essential is that *information* should be widely available. The more available it is, the better markets work. However, the very nature of information – being personal and local – often makes this hard to achieve. Often the cost of getting market information isn't worth the gain: the same new television may be cheaper in another store, but is it really worth going round them all to check?

It is hard to create a system of property rights from scratch.

The fourth essential is *property* and the rights that go with it – to hold it, enjoy its products, exclude others from it and buy or sell it as you choose. The rules of property are not straightforward – in England for example, you can cut down the overhanging branches of neighbours' trees, provided that you offer them the wood back – because it can take centuries to hammer out a system that everyone is happy with. As Russia found, you can't easily create a system of property rights from scratch. This makes it hard to create markets afresh.

The fifth essential for a successful market is *competition*. Markets work best where customers have a choice of providers to buy from. It encourages innovation and diversity, and helps customers to find exactly what they need.

Competition also demands that people must be relatively free to set up as rivals to existing suppliers (or, indeed, enter the market as new customers). Again, competition is likely to be less strong in thinly populated areas, or where governments impose costly regulations that new, small firms can't afford.

> **You cannot have a thriving market if some participants are above the law.**

All this implies the need for proper *enforcement* of the rules. For markets to work, property must be protected from trespass and theft, coercion and corruption must be outlawed and contracts must be honoured. The enforcement must also apply equally to all: you cannot have a thriving market if some of its participants are above the law or bend it to suit themselves.

But the law is a last resort, and sometimes an expensive one. If people are to conduct everyday exchanges, they must have the sixth market essential: *trust* in the process and in the people they are dealing with. Markets have ways of creating a basis of trust; but again, it can take many years for them to develop.

I would say, then, that there is a seventh essential for markets to work well, and that is *culture*. In free economies, people are so steeped in the everyday workings of the market that it is like a language to them. They pick up and understand its rules, just as they understand grammar, without being taught – without even being able to explain what the rules are. They soon become fluent, in ways that it takes non-natives years to match, if they ever do. And it's as hard to become fluent in a language as it is to become fluent in markets.

GROWING MARKETS OVER THE NET

If you can get all these ingredients together, you can grow markets in the most unlikely places. Like cyberspace.

The online auction company eBay, founded in 1995, made billionaires of its principals, Pierre Omidyar and Jeff Skoll. You can buy or sell just about anything on eBay (one

Australian prankster once tried to sell New Zealand: the price was up to $3000 before eBay closed down the sale). It's now quite vast. But as in other markets, similar items are grouped together so you don't have to trawl through thousands of antiques, books, carpets, coins, phones, stamps or Cabbage Patch Kids, just to find the Ford Edsel you always wanted.

Participants can sell items at a fixed price (one sold her DJ husband's Lotus Elise for a dollar after she heard him flirting with another woman over the airwaves), but it is best known as an online auction. Its great edge over a physical auction is that time and geography are less of a barrier: you can trade with people in the dead of night, on the far side of the planet.

The wider the market, the more useful and efficient it is; and online markets are as big as they come. My old business of selling antique prints has turned into my current hobby, collecting them. This used to mean many hours looking around old bookshops in the hope of picking up one of the few specific items I was searching for. Now I can search thousands of sellers online without moving from my keyboard.

THE QUESTION OF ONLINE TRUST

With the whole online world as potential sellers or buyers, how can participants in this market ever establish the trust needed to make it work? How do I know that the prints I buy will be in good condition—or that they will even arrive? How can sellers be sure that I will actually pay them?

In fact, eBay has developed a number of mechanisms to ensure that people feel safe in its market place. Buyers and sellers all have to sign up to eBay's market rules. Their rights are posted online. Toolbars alert users to potential frauds. Chatrooms debate any worries. And sellers can post a photograph of the goods, enabling buyers like me, who are very interested in the condition of their antique print, to check it first.

The most famous trust-building feature is the online feedback system.

Yet eBay's most famous trust-building feature is the online feedback system, in which buyers and sellers can rate each other, giving a score to indicate how reliable (or otherwise) they were. Buy from a seller with positive ratings from lots of customers, and you can be reasonably sure that you won't be cheated. For sellers anywhere, good customer feedback is always important, because it encourages new buyers to do business: online, where customers don't have the body-language information of a face-to-face market, it is absolutely vital.

This online market succeeds, partly because it is fun – the last-minute cat-and-mouse bidding as the auction closes has been likened to the thrill of gambling – but more because it embodies all the market essentials. There is worldwide competition among both buyers and sellers; it is voluntary; it maintains and enforces rules to protect participants' property; it has found ways to promote trust. It even seems to have developed a sort of online market culture of its own.

THE SLOW GROWTH OF THE MARKET IN CHINA

So you need to have the right conditions in place for markets to grow well, and to spread the benefits of free exchange to everyone involved. Corruption, violence, monopolies, barriers against new competitors, poor information – all these make it hard for markets to prosper. But like weeds growing through the concrete, markets seem able to take root and survive almost anywhere.

Which brings me back to China.

China may not seem very fertile ground in which to grow markets. Like Russia, it has endured decades of communism, which replaced a largely peasant economy. But unlike Russia, China still calls itself communist. If markets can survive here, they can survive anywhere.

And yet China is gradually growing into a market economy – more slowly than Russia, but perhaps more certainly. Its reforms have been gradual. They started with the family responsibility system, replacing the collective farms. The land is still technically owned in common, but now each family reaps the harvest that they sow, which seems little different from private ownership. No wonder production boomed.

Prices have been liberalized, but *gradually*, which has helped limit disruption. Production too has been liberalized, but instead of being sold wholesale, firms have been restructured, and given incentives to perform better. State production quotas have remained, but workers have been allowed to keep the profits from any additional production. Not surprisingly, production is, again, booming.

Meanwhile, new local enterprises have been formed – village enterprises that will soon dominate China's economy. But the gradual pace has allowed the old economic relationships and trust to persist, even as new ones spring up. And with China's draconian rule of law, people can be more certain of trading securely than can any Russian.

> *The only salvation of the world today . . . is the rapid dissemination of the basic values of the West, that is, the ideas of democracy, human rights, the civil society, and the free market.*
> **– Former Czech president Vaclav Havel**

THE ONLY REAL WAY TO WEALTH

China is growing. It's not yet rich, yet with its careful nurturing of the market economy, it looks set to become so. Yes, there is still too much government control, and too much repression: but prices are starting to take over the work of central planners, individuals can now enjoy the rewards of hard work and enterprise, people are building up new capital, corruption is being squeezed out and new trading relationships are growing. And all this, even within a (nominally) communist country.

I often think about my black-haired Lanzhou seamstress. I imagine she had worked long hours in some sweatshop to raise the money she needed for what she really wanted – to run her own business. I like to believe that by now she has earned enough from her enterprise to get a sewing machine for herself and maybe take on an employee. Perhaps one day she will be running a successful clothing business, and, on the other side of the world, I will buy her products. If so, I probably won't realize it, because although the market enabled us to cooperate to our mutual advantage, I could not even speak enough of her language to discover her name.

But however she fares, I'm sure it won't be income redistribution, nor the communism of the past, that will raise her and hundreds of millions like her out of poverty. It will be hard work, customer service, luck, incentives, ambition and enterprise.

It will be the *market*.

Index